WITHDRAWN

EDWARD KING AND MARTYR

CHRISTINE E. FELL
Lecturer in English Language
and
Medieval English Literature
University of Leeds

THE UNIVERSITY OF LEEDS
SCHOOL OF ENGLISH
1971

© Christine E. Fell

PRINTED IN GREAT BRITAIN BY THE SCOLAR PRESS LTD.
20 MAIN STREET, MENSTON, YORKS., ENGLAND

ACKNOWLEDGMENTS

I am grateful to the President and Fellows of St John's College Oxford, and to the Master and Fellows of Corpus Christi College Cambridge for permission to publish material from their manuscripts. Whenever I have consulted texts, asked for information or requested photostats from these colleges, from the British Museum and the Bodleian Library, or from the libraries of Lambeth Palace, York Minster, Trinity College Dublin, Cardiff and Gotha, I have received most courteous help. My colleagues at Leeds have patiently answered my questions in a variety of disciplines, Professor P. H. Sawyer and Mrs Pauline Stafford on charters, Mr R. H. Martin and Mr R. L. Thomson on medieval Latin, Mr J. R. Wilkie and Dr C. D. M. Cossar on German catalogues. Dr G. R. Rastall has transcribed and described the music of MS CCCC 371. Professor A. C. Cawley has read my typescript with his customary editorial thoroughness. For information on liturgy from Mr C. Hohler of the Courtauld Institute I am also grateful. My thanks are chiefly due to Dr R. I. Page of Corpus Christi College Cambridge, whose critical attention, given to both first and final drafts, has preserved me from many over-confident statements.

CHRISTINE E. FELL

CONTENTS

INTRODUCTION

I.	Bibliographical Material	.. ..	iii
II.	Manuscripts of the *Passio* ..	.. ..	v
III.	Printed texts of the *Passio*	.. ..	xi
IV.	Vernacular versions of the *Passio*..	.. .. ..	xiv
V.	Chronicles ..	.. ..	xvi
VI.	Sources of the *Passio*	.. ..	xvii
VII.	Author of the *Passio*	.. ..	xx
VIII.	Development of the cult of St Edward	.. .. ..	xx

Notes	.. ..	xxv
List of manuscripts ..	.. ..	xxix

TEXT

Appendix A	Text of hymn to Edward in MS BM Harley 1117 ..	17
Appendix B	Text and music of hymns to Edward in MS Cambridge Corpus Christi 371	18
Plate	MS Corpus Christi 371 f.3r	21

i

INTRODUCTION

It is reasonable to say that the confusion surrounding the death in 978 of Edward King and Martyr has been created by twentieth-century scholarship as much as by the circumstances of his murder. The most elaborate exposition of the material is in Dr C. E. Wright's *The Cultivation of Saga in Anglo-Saxon England*[1]. Dr Wright traces the development of stories about the martyrdom from the brief entry in the *Anglo-Saxon Chronicle*[2] and the first detailed account in the anonymous *Vita Oswaldi*[3] through the variants as they occur in the Latin chronicles. As he discusses each chronicle he points out which part of the material is new, and uses the accumulation and variation of detail as evidence for his theory of the existence of saga-telling and saga-development.

A similar interpretation is offered in briefer form by Professor R. M. Wilson in *The Lost Literature of Medieval England*[4]. Here Professor Wilson summarizes the variations and draws the conclusion that "These different versions indicate that there must have been in circulation many stories dealing with the death of Edward which are known to-day only from the later Latin writings." The texts to which Dr Wright and Professor Wilson refer, apart from the *Anglo-Saxon Chronicle* and the *Vita Oswaldi*, are the chronicles of Florence of Worcester, Henry of Huntingdon, William of Malmesbury, Walter Map and Gaimar. To this list Professor Wilson adds Osbern's *Vita Dunstani* and a reference by Wulfstan in *Sermo Lupi*. Dr Wright refers to two more, John of Wallingford's *Chronica* and the Icelandic *Dunstanus Saga*[5].

The main criticism of both Dr Wright's and Professor Wilson's position is that they have examined the chronicles without appearing to have realized that a life of St Edward exists. It is not easy to see why the *Passio et Miracula Sancti Eadwardi Regis et Martyris* has been overlooked, not only by them, but also by historians dealing with the reign of Edward. It is found in manuscript and print, and it turns up in many and various forms, in liturgy, in chronicle and in vernacular legendary. Before it has been examined and its place in the Edward material ascertained, discussion of the development of legends about Edward is necessarily based on inadequate evidence.

I. Bibliographical Material

The *Passio Sancti Eadwardi* is not omitted from recent bibliography and catalogue. The *Bibliotheca Hagiographica Latina*[6] mentions it, and refers to Hardy's *Catalogue*[7] for a description of the manuscripts. Hardy lists five manuscripts under the heading *Passio Sancti Eadwardi Regis et Martyris, subjuncta miraculorum relatione*. Before examining these manuscripts in detail it is convenient to see what other Edward material is listed in bibliography and catalogue. The *Bibliotheca* has four entries:

(i) *Passio et Miracula*. This is printed in shortened form by Surius, and Surius's version is used by the Bollandists in the *Acta Sanctorum*[8].
(ii) Capgrave[9].
(iii) John of Brompton's *Chronicle*[10], also used by the Bollandists.
(iv) Petrus de Natalibus[11].

Of these four the first is the *Passio* itself, the second and third are variant forms of the *Passio*. The fourth is a slight and late contribution, little more than a paragraph, the details of which indicate both the *Passio* and the *Anglo-Saxon Chronicle* as ultimate source material.

Hardy's *Catalogue* has six entries:

(i) Five manuscripts of the *Passio:* BM Add.11,881; St. John's Oxford, 96; Bodleian Rawlinson A 903; Bodleian Rawlinson C 440; BM Lansdowne 436. The reference to Rawlinson A 903 is erroneous. There is only one Rawlinson manuscript containing the *Passio*. It appears in the "Old List" as A 903 and in the current catalogue as C 440.[12]

(ii) *Narratio de S. Edwardo* existing in only one manuscript, Bodleian Digby 146. On investigation this proves to be an incomplete manuscript of the *Passio*, not a distinct text.

(iii) *De Sancto Edwardo, Rege et Martyre* for which Hardy gives two manuscript references BM Cotton Tiberius E 1, and Bodleian Tanner 15. He comments: "Printed in Capgrave's 'Legenda Nova Angliae,' f.116. It appears to be an abridgement of MS Addit 11,881 in the British Museum." This is the Capgrave version of the *Passio*, listed also in the *Bibliotheca*. There is a third manuscript of it which Hardy does not mention, but to which Horstmann draws our attention in his edition of Capgrave, regretting that he has been unable to consult it.[13] This is York Cathedral Library MS XVI C 1. In fact the York manuscript is very closely related to Tanner 15, and this group of manuscripts shares with the early printed text of Capgrave an almost identical version of the *Passio* with no independent variants. There is no obvious reason why Hardy should have specified a relationship with Additional, since the Capgrave version shares certain slight variants not with Additional but with Rawlinson and Lansdowne.

(iv) *Vita S. Eduardi, Regis Anglorum, carmine conscripta Gallico et Latino*. Hardy lists one manuscript, Bibl. Regin. Sueciae in Vaticana 1292. He takes his information here from the author of the *Histoire littéraire de la France* who in rhetorical and patriotic tone ascribes the work to Abbo of Fleury on the somewhat dubious grounds that it has the air of being "la production d'une plume Françoise" and that Abbo was in England shortly after the death of Edward the Martyr. Had he read the poem with attention he might have discovered that it was not about Edward the Martyr but Edward the Confessor. Hardy lists it again with a different manuscript reference, Vatic. Christin. 489 when he is dealing with Confessor material.[14] The error must have arisen from the existence of two separate catalogue systems for the Vatican collection of Queen Christina's manuscripts. The recently re-issued catalogue[15] makes it clear that Montfaucon

1292 = Reg. Lat. 489.

(v) *Versus de translatione corporis S. Eadwardi, Regis et Martyris*. This is a twenty-six line poem in BM Harley 1117.

(vi) *Life of St Edward, King and Martyr*. This, the Middle English life of St Edward in the *South English Legendary*, is a close translation of the *Passio*, as I shall demonstrate later.

The only one of these entries which is non-*Passio* material is item (v) the poem in Harley 1117. Apart from this we have:

(i) Four manuscripts of the *Passio:* (ii) A further manuscript of the *Passio:* (iii) An abbreviated version of the *Passio:* (iv) An erroneous reference: (vi) A translation of the *Passio*.

Hardy follows his bibliographical material with a short commentary. He says that the unknown author of the *Passio* lived about the end of the eleventh century and may have been Eadmer. The dating is probably accurate, the ascription to Eadmer probably not. Hardy comments further that there is a life of Edward in John of Brompton's *Chronicle*. This, (see above, p.iv) is not a separate version, but a text of the *Passio*.

II. MANUSCRIPTS OF THE PASSIO

Four manuscripts still extant which Hardy did not locate are:
(i) Cardiff Public Library 1.381
(ii) Gotha Landesbibliothek Memb. I 81
(iii) Trinity College Dublin 171
(iv) Lambeth Palace Library 149
This gives a total of nine. There may of course be others which I have not traced.

BM Additional 11,881 (A)

Additional is a twelfth-century folio manuscript for which we have no provenance. It is a collection of saints' lives in which Edward occurs between St John, Abbot, and St Gregory, Pope. The manuscript is imperfect, having been mutilated by the removal of pages and of illuminated initials. Though it is clear that it originally contained the complete text of both *Passio* and *Miracula*, the entire description of the martyrdom is now missing, and most of the remaining pages are damaged.

Cardiff Public Library 1.381 (C)

This is a mid-twelfth-century manuscript, containing the complete *Passio et Miracula Eadwardi*, although, unlike the other manuscripts, it does not use this terminology, preferring the title *Vita beati Regis Edwardi*. It is again a collection of saints' lives in which Edward's comes after St Hildelitha's and before that of his sister St Edith, both the work of the hagiographer Goscelin. Neil Ker[17] assigns the manuscript without absolute certainty to the abbey of the Blessed Virgin Mary and St Ethelburga, a convent of Benedictine nuns, at Barking, Essex. Marvin L. Colker, writing on "Texts of Jocelyn of Canterbury,"[18] suggests that the first item certainly, and the whole codex possibly, had once belonged to St Martin's priory, Dover.

The manuscript contains a full and excellent text of the *Passio et Miracula* to which a later hand has added a number of marginalia. Most of these lack interest, as they merely duplicate information in the text. At 1,3 for example the marginal comment is *Dunstanus archipraesul*, at 3,22 *dyabolus*, at 9,26 *c. hiddas terre*. The only dramatic one is at 5,9 ff. where, as the murderer prepares to stab Edward, the words (*i*)*udas scarioth* occur in the margin above a gracefully delineated hand with the index finger extended.

Trinity College Dublin 171 (Db)

This is a thirteenth-century manuscript containing the complete *Passio et Miracula Eadwardi*. It contains saints' lives in approximate calendar order, Edward following Gertrude, Virgin, and preceding John, Confessor. It was formerly the property of the Cistercian abbey of the Blessed Virgin Mary at Jervaulx, Yorkshire.

Bodleian Digby 146 (Dy)

Here the *Passio* only, not the *Miracula*, is found at the end of an eleventh-century quarto manuscript of the works of Aldhelm. It appears to be a separate manuscript which has been bound together with the Aldhelm, and is likely to have the same provenance, that is the Benedictine abbey of the Blessed Virgin Mary at Abingdon, Berkshire.

The *Passio* is written in a twelfth-century hand, untidy and inaccurate, and there are spaces for initials which have not been illuminated. The material on Edgar is omitted, Dy beginning with the accession of Edward, and ending with the building of a church on the site of Edward's first posthumous miracle, the healing of a blind woman who watched over his corpse the night after the murder. It lacks, therefore, the transference of the body to Wareham and its later translation to Shaftesbury.

Hardy's comment on this manuscript is that the *Passio* "ends abruptly at the beginning of a chapter." Certainly it ends where he says it does with the words "(N)isi granum frumenti" but these words are not part of the *Passio* text. They are the opening words of St John's Gospel XII,24, and form one of the antiphons sung *in vigilia unius martyris*. This, together with the division of Dy into eight paragraphs of approximately equal length, a paragraphing not shared by the other manuscripts, suggests that it was intended for use as the lections to be read on St Edward's day. It is worth noting that Abingdon, having been granted land by Edward, and claiming some of his relics, naturally held him in high honour.[19]

Gotha Landesbibliothek Memb. I 81 (G)

The Gotha manuscript is described in the catalogue of that library as thirteenth-century, by Marvin Colker as mid-fifteenth-century.[20] The disparity between these dates suggested that the manuscript might be in different hands, but a letter from the librarian of the Landesbibliothek assures me that except for f.1r the manuscript is in one hand throughout, and that hand certainly not fifteenth-century: "Dem Schriftcharakter nach ist sie wahrscheinlich dem Ende des 13. Jahrhunderts, eher noch dem 14. Jahrhundert zuzuweisen."

G contains the *Passio* not the *Miracula* of Edward, and within the *Passio* some but not all of the early material on Edgar is omitted. It is a manuscript written by a fairly unintelligent or uninformed scribe, containing a higher proportion of nonsensical variants than any of the other manuscripts. Nothing appears to be known of the provenance, but it is a collection of saints' lives including Edward among many other English ones. It has a rich collection of marginalia, some of them simply indicative of content, as at 8,28 *de sancta Eadgith filia regis Eadgar*. A geographical one at 7,10 tells us, accurately enough, that Bere is in the province of Dorset, ten miles from Wareham, fifteen from Shaftesbury. An almost indecipherable annotation occurs against the account of the murder. Most of the words disappear into the binding, but those that can be read appear to include *equus*, *cestre* and *ephi* . . . (*epiphium*, *ephipium* "saddle"). It is likely that the information offered is the same as Gaimar's — that, as Edward fell, his horse galloped away towards Cirencester where the saddle may yet be seen.[21] Towards the end of the *Passio* the margin is filled with prayers, culminating in the *Deus aeterne triumphator*, a prayer from the Mass for St Edward's day.[22]

Lambeth Palace Library 149 (Lb)

The Lambeth manuscript belongs to the late twelfth or early thirteenth century and comes from the Augustine priory of the Blessed Virgin Mary and St John the Baptist at Lanthony, Gloucestershire. This is not a collection of saints' lives, and the *Passio Eadwardi* comes between the *Enchiridion* of St Augustine and Augustine *de penitencia*. It has a complete text of the *Passio et Miracula*, containing a number of minor additions to the text as found in the other manuscripts. These additions are unlikely to be the work of the scribe of Lb, who is a meticulously accurate copyist, correcting his errors even when they are merely transpositional, and at 4,11 unnecessarily correcting his aberrant *uocatur* to *dicitur*. It is probable therefore that most of the additions and alterations which characterize Lb existed in the manuscript from which it was copied.

BM Lansdowne 436 (Ln)

Lansdowne is a fourteenth-century manuscript from the abbey of the Blessed Virgin Mary and St Elfleda, a convent of Benedictine nuns at Romsey, Hampshire. It is a collection of the lives of English saints, arranged alphabetically, *Edwardus Martyr* coming between Edburga and Erkenwaldus. It contains the *Passio* only, not the *Miracula*, and large portions of the *Passio* itself are omitted. It is a handsome, ornamental volume, with careful red and blue initialling.

Bodleian Rawlinson C 440 (R)

Rawlinson is a Cistercian abbey manuscript, possibly from the diocese of York, but apparently in the possession of Henry Spelman and therefore in Norfolk in the sixteenth century. The catalogue describes it as twelfth-century, but Mr R. W. Hunt of the Bodleian tells me that the main part of the manuscript cannot be earlier than the second quarter of the thirteenth century. It contains saints' lives but in no obvious order, Edward coming between Longinus and Olaf; and though St Edmund is also represented, the manuscript has a cosmopolitan rather than an insular emphasis. There is a complete text of both *Passio* and *Miracula* in R. They are rather carelessly written, but the scribe has a well-organized system of inserting corrections.

One of the most interesting features of R is the calendar prefixed to the manuscript, taken from another smaller manuscript in the same monastic library. This calendar indicates the various volumes in the library which contain the appropriate *historiae* for the feast days. R's own library number is G iii. A marginal note explains how the system operates:
"Istud kalendarium servit tantummodo de vitis et passionibus sanctorum inveniendis in diversis libris scriptis. Primo cursum littere, postea numerum librorum exterius scriptum qui voluerit querat, et sic inveniet."

St. John's Oxford, 96 (Sj)

This is a handsome folio manuscript of the twelfth century, which was originally the property of the Benedictine abbey of St Edburga (formerly of the Blessed Virgin Mary, St Peter and St Paul) at Pershore, Worcestershire. It contains material on four saints only, the *Vita et Miracula* of Oswald and of Mary Magdalene, the *Passio et Miracula* of Edward, and *De Augustini in Anglia aduentu* by Goscelin. In the life of St Oswald marginal corrections occur, but there are practically no corrections throughout the *Passio* even of obvious errors such as dittography. In fairness it should be said that there are very few errors.

Manuscript relations

Five of the manuscripts contain complete texts of both *Passio* and *Miracula*. These are C Db Lb R and Sj. Of these Db Lb and R are probably later than the other two, C and Sj being certainly twelfth-century. Of the remaining four, the incomplete manuscripts of which A alone is incomplete by accident not design, A and Dy are twelfth-century, G and Ln much later.

Sj, as well as being complete and early, appears also to be the most reliable manuscript, and it is the one from which I have transcribed my basic text. I have normalized the punctuation, use of capitals and paragraphs, and also the orthography except in the case of proper names. Thus Sj's ę in *pręsul*, *cępit* and *ęcclesia*, is given variously as *praesul*, *coepit* and *ecclesia;* i/y variants in *martir/ martyr* and *himnus/hymnus* are rendered consistently as y; omission or assimilation of consonants as in *stemate*, *extirparet*, *sulleuemur* are regularized in *stemmate, exstirparet, subleuemur;* c and t are distinguished, and less familiar spellings such as *flagrantia* for *fragrantia* are replaced by the more immediately recognisable forms.

This account is selective, not comprehensive, and applies only to Sj. In the variants from other manuscripts I have ignored all purely orthographical ones, unless they seemed to have some special interest, e.g. Lb's *Wiltun* for *Wiltonia* 8,24 where the spelling indicates the English form of the name. In listing variants I have avoided normalizing the spelling, except in giving *ae* for *ę*, with the result that occasionally there appears to be a greater discrepancy than actually exists between Sj and the other manuscripts. Nevertheless this seemed preferable to any attempt to normalize variants, since one cannot normalize errors.

The only alterations I have made in the wording of Sj are, with four exceptions, where all the other manuscripts combine to give a different reading. These occur at 3,14; 4,19; 4,22; 6,18-19; 10,22; 11,20; 12,3 and 15,28. Most of them are quite obviously erroneous, even without the evidence of the other manuscripts, being simple mistakes of grammar, omission or dittography. The exceptions are Sj's *circuiret* 14,22, a reading shared by Db only; *dispersi* 4,22 shared by C; *flore* omitted from Sj 3,19 but necessary to the sense, is inserted from Lb, the only manuscript in which it is found; and Sj's *delicias* 13,6, shared by the majority of the manuscripts, is replaced by *reliquias* from Db and Lb. The scribes of Db and Lb here were presumably copying or restoring an original reading. Sj's only variant of interest is at 4,19, where the scribe in a moment of aberration describes Corfe Castle as *celeste* rather than *celebre*.

Apart from orthographical ones, I have listed all variants from all manuscripts, and included variants from the printed texts, John of Brompton, Capgrave and the lectionaries, only where these were informative. From a comparison of the variants it becomes clear that A Db and Sj are very closely related. There are five occasions where these three alone share a reading against all other manuscripts, and since so much of A is missing, this figure is based on approximately two-thirds of the text. There are a number of other occasions where these three, together with C or Ln or both, form a group against the remaining manuscripts. The similarity between the three is so close that it seems possible that they were transcribed from the same manuscript. That Db and Sj share the reading *circuiret* is suggestive, and it is worth noting that Db is from Yorkshire and Sj from Worcestershire, even though there had ceased to be an official link between the sees of Worcester and York by the twelfth century. The connexion between the group is strengthened by the fact that A and Db share almost the same wording for the Introduction to the *Passio* and later to the *Miracula* where the majority of the manuscripts behave independently.

Against the group A Db Sj are almost always found G Lb and R. There is also one occasion where G and R alone share an odd and erroneous reading (1,2). C and Ln are sometimes found supporting the A Db Sj group of readings, sometimes the G Lb R group, and sometimes one is found on either side. Dy on the other hand is almost invariably independent.

This pattern could be illustrated by a conjectural stemma, in which the letter x would represent hypothetical manuscripts, and a broken line would

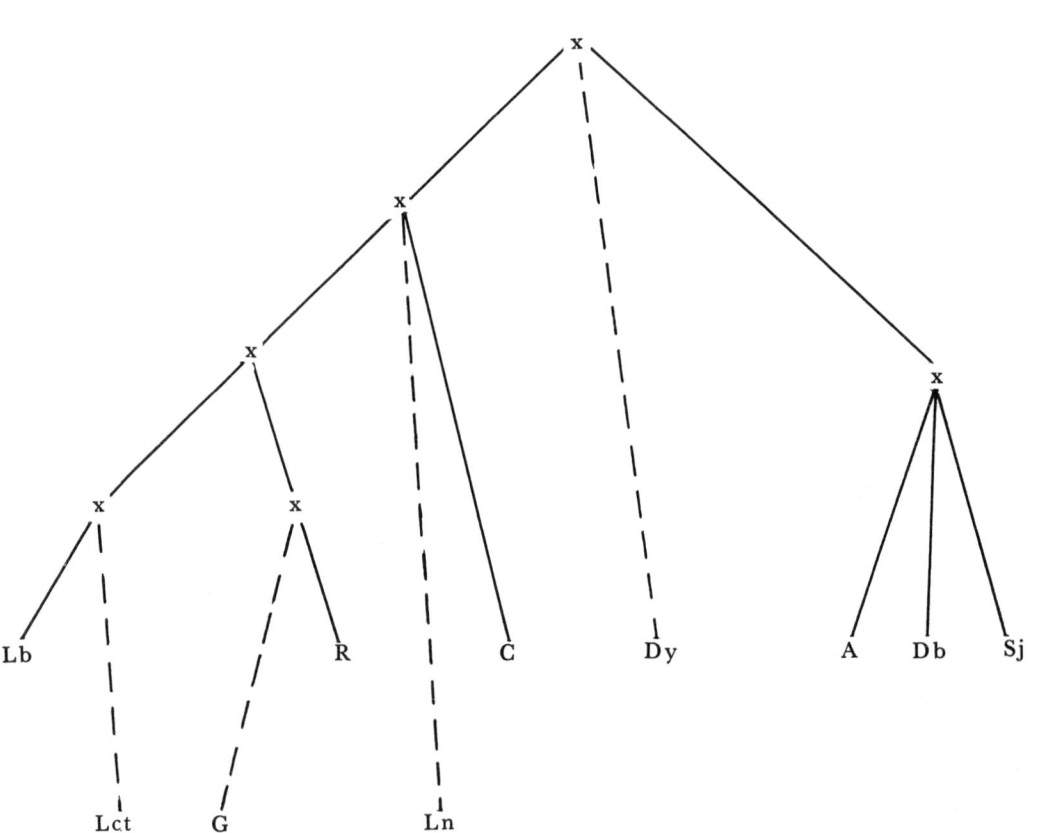

indicate the probability of a number of intervening ones. The abbreviation Lct is used for the lectionary variants; see below p. xiii.

But any stemma represents a possibility rather than a probability, in that to avoid multiplying hypothetical manuscripts one looks for the simplest way of relating the surviving ones, whereas in reality the relationships are likely to have been a good deal more complex with a greater number of intervening exemplars. Moreover, though the general groupings of the manuscripts are clear, there are odd occasions where the pattern is broken. As mentioned, Db and Lb share the reading *reliquias* not *delicias* at 13,6, and C and R share *co-aeterno* not *aeterno* at 16,4. Such similarities do not necessarily indicate that these manuscripts are related. The scribe's own judgement may have been at work on the first of these, and the second is a familiar variant of a traditional formula.

However, three things emerge clearly from the comparison. One is the presence of two separate groups of manuscripts, A Db Sj and G Lb R, with an intermediary group C Ln, and a single independent manuscript, Dy. It is also clear that A Db Sj represent a more closely-knit group than the other, and may well be nearer to the prototype. Thirdly, it is evident that none of the manuscripts has been copied from any other surviving one, since each has a number of independent readings which are not duplicated elsewhere.

There are very few interesting variants of meaning as distinct from errors. Dy is alone in its statement that Edward's reign was three years seven months, not three years eight months. Dy also makes Edward's murderer the one who offered him the cup, *poculum*, rather than the kiss, *osculum*. And at 2,21 where the bishops are variously *religiosis*, *religionis* and *regionis*, the scribe of Dy sensibly leaves them unqualified. The original, doubtless, had an indecipherable abbreviation. A significant variant is Db's substitution at 1,11 of *Oswaldo Wigornensi* for *Æthelwoldo Wintoniensi*. This must be an alteration not an original reading. Db is the Jervaulx manuscript, and it may be that Oswald, bishop of Worcester, archbishop of York, was more highly regarded in northern dioceses than Æthelwold of Winchester. It is perhaps worth noting that the John of Brompton text of the *Passio* inserts *cum sancto Oswaldo Eboracensi archiepiscopo* after *eumque* at 2,20 where Edward's coronation by Dunstan is described. John of Brompton was of course abbot of Jervaulx, and though he is not considered the compiler of the chronicle that bears his name, he may have had a hand in the redaction which survives.[23]

III. PRINTED TEXTS OF THE PASSIO (a)

There are a number of early printed texts which contain versions of the *Passio*. The *Bibliotheca* and *Catalogue* have already drawn our attention to three. These are Capgrave's *Nova Legenda Angliae*, Surius's *De Probatis Sanctorum Historiis*, and John of Brompton's *Chronicle*.

Capgrave's Nova Legenda Angliae *(NLA)*

The opening of the *NLA*, a brief summary of Edward's succession to the throne and the circumstances of his election and coronation, is probably but not demonstrably a summary of the first part of the *Passio*. The material corresponds approximately to *Passio* text 2,15-21. But when the *NLA* describes Edward's martyrdom it follows the *Passio* very closely:

Passio 5,4   blande eum et amicabiliter salutat, ad hospitium inuitat
NLA 349,20   blande eum salutat et ad suum hospitium inuitat.

The *NLA* follows the account of the murder, with more material from the *Passio* concerning the cure of the blind woman, the miraculous column of fire, the body's translation to Shaftesbury, and its change of resting-place in the year 1001 AD. A sentence not from the *Passio* tells us of the stepmother's expiation of her crime in founding the monasteries at Wherwell and Amesbury.

There are two places where the *NLA* supports individual manuscripts of the *Passio*. At 12,7 it shares with R *in sompnis* against the *in uisione* of all other manuscripts. At 13,6 the *NLA ad locum decentiorem* must derive from a manuscript which shared Ln's *decenter* for *diligenter*.

Surius's De Probatis Sanctorum Historiis

The abbreviated version of the *Passio* printed by Surius is different from and fuller than Capgrave's. It is much less close to the *Passio* verbally, and not demonstrably related to any one manuscript. It is, however, demonstrably related to the *Passio* as a whole. Surius has more of the early material on both Edgar and Edward. He also includes the story of Ethelred's grief for his brother's death, and his mother's consequent violence, *Passio* 7,13 to 19, material not utilized by Capgrave. The following sentence is reasonably representative in showing how Surius follows the *Passio* closely in sense and sequence but diverges in vocabulary:

Passio 3,20   castitate laudabilis, facie decorus et hilaris, consilio et prudentia probatissimus
Surius 277   castitate venerabilem, facie iucundem & decorum, consilio & prudentia spectatissimum.

John of Brompton's Chronicle *(JB)*

JB starts with an introductory summarizing sentence, and then goes straight into *Passio* transcription. His second sentence corresponds to *Passio* 2,17 *Sed dum consecrationis*, and he then follows the *Passio* almost word for word as far as 11,21 *sanitati restituta est*. The only slight divergences within this area are occasional omissions of sentences, but these do not correspond to any of the manuscript ommissions. *JB* for example omits 3,17 to 21 a sentence in all manuscripts of the *Passio*, but includes the preceding material which is omitted from Ln or Dy. *JB* also provides some additional material taken ultimately from the *Anglo-Saxon Chronicle*. He mentions the appearance of the comet, and follows his *Passio* transcription with information about the councils at Calne during Edward's reign. For the benefit of uninformed readers he explains *Septoniam* as *id est Schaftesbiry*, and he shares with other chroniclers and with Capgrave the story of Ælfthryth's expiatory founding of monasteries.

Printed texts of the Passio (b) Breviaries

The survey so far has covered most of the items mentioned by *Bibliotheca* and *Catalogue*, but neither of these two draw our attention to liturgy. In the *Acta Sanctorum*, however, where both the Surius and the *JB* texts are printed, the editors note the similarity between *JB* and the Salisbury breviary lections. This similarity, naturally enough, is because the breviary lessons for St Edward's day are taken from the *Passio*.

I am not including here an exhaustive study of the lectionary variants, but it is worthwhile indicating some of the ways in which the lessons for St Edward's day in different breviaries relate to each other and to the *Passio*. Basically there are two versions, that of the Salisbury breviary, and that of the Hyde Abbey breviary.

Salisbury breviary

This redaction of the *Passio* is shared by the Salisbury breviary, the Exeter breviary and the thirteenth-century lectionary BM Cotton Appendix XXIII.[24] In these three the text is from the *Passio* 3,1 *Sanctus Eadwardus* to 6,4 *diiudicandus erit*, but within this framework there is a slight variation in that the lessons do not begin and end at identical points.

These three sets of lessons vary little from the *Passio* and less from each other. They share a number of Lb's readings and minor additions, and these are noted in the manuscript variants. Since there are minor errors in Lb that they do not share, it seems probable that they and Lb derive from the same prototype, not that Lb itself is the source. Moreover there are a number of variants which are common to the three sets of lections, but are not shared by Lb or by any other basic manuscript of the *Passio*. Examples are *Mox impiissima regina* for *cum illa rursum* at 5,6, *scelus* instead of *scilicet* at 5,8, and *major* not *immanior* at 5,10. It is clear that these three texts represent a single redaction of the *Passio*, and that this redaction is very closely related to Lb.

Hyde Abbey breviary *(HA)*

The monastic breviary of Hyde Abbey (New Minster, Winchester) has eight lessons for St Edward's day. These are taken from the *Passio*, but from a much more extensive area of the *Passio* than are the preceding lections. The Salisbury version starts with Edward's accession and ends with his death. *HA* contains in the first *lectio* material on Edgar, Dunstan and Edward's coronation, reaches Edward's death by the end of *lectio* four, and spends the remaining four lessons on posthumous miracle, discovery of the body, and translation.

Much of *HA* is verbally identical with the *Passio* text, but there is one striking innovation. Within the precise verbal framework of the original, a single phrase is altered to underline the Queen's responsibility for the murder:

Passio 5,13 Nam postquam poculum a pincerna suscipiens summo tenus ore attigit, is qui osculum sibi intulerat, ex aduerso insiliens, cultello mox eius uiscera transfixit.

HA Postquam autem poculum a pincerna suscipiens summo tenus ore attigit.| quidam maligne mulieris instinctu ex aduerso insiliens cultello mox eius uiscera transfixit.

Printed texts of the Passio (c)

An almost exact transcription of Sj was made by W. H. Hutton and printed together with his lectures on *The English Saints*.[25] It is a transcription made without reference to other manuscripts, and with selective indication of scribal error. The lecture speaks movingly of the boy-king who spurned the coarse vices of his age, but adds little to our knowledge of him.

IV. VERNACULAR VERSIONS OF THE PASSIO

There are two important translations of the *Passio*. One which Dr Wright noted though he did not recognize its source is that in the Icelandic *Dunstanus Saga*. In the Introduction to my edition of that saga I was able to demonstrate that so far from being a distorted and unreliable version of the legend, the saga contained direct translation of the *Passio*. In addition to the Icelandic vernacular version there is item (vi) in Hardy's *Catalogue*, the Middle English life of St Edward contained in the *South English Legendary* (*SEL*).

The *SEL* story of Edward opens with the statement which it shares only with Dy that Edward reigned for three years seven months. One of the *SEL* manuscripts changes the seven months to eight days. At first the translator paraphrases rather than translating directly, and adds occasional pieces of proverbial wisdom such as "stepmoder is selde god". But when he moves on to description of Edward himself the translation becomes closer:

Passio 3,20 cunctis erat affabilis, castitate laudabilis, facie decorus et hilaris, consilio et prudentia probatissimus.

SEL 16 He was meok & milde inou. & fair of fleiss & felle
Deboner to speke wiþ. and wiþ pouere men mest
Chast and wis of conseil.

Directly translated also are details such as the diabolical instigation of the stepmother's hatred, and Edward's wish, when he was out hunting, to go and see his brother at Corfe. However, it is not in the general outline of the story that we have the most convincing proof of the *Legendary*'s debt to the *Passio* but in the irrelevancies:

Passio 4,18 in loco qui ab incolis Corph nuncupatur, a uilla memorata tribus milibus distans, ubi nunc castrum satis celebre constructum est.

SEL 48 In a toun þat me clupede Corf. þat bote þreo mile nas
A strong castel þer is nou. ac þo nas þar non þere.

The details of the murder are the same in the two texts, except that the *SEL* has an additional statement in one manuscript about the actual knife used, a long and narrow one apparently, which we are told may yet be seen in Caversham church.²⁶ After this the author of the *SEL* digresses to speak of Ethelred in terms which he claims to draw from the life of St Alphe, better known as Ælfheah or Elphege. He then returns to his primary source the *Passio* for the description of Edward's translation to Shaftesbury, St Edith's dramatic reception of the body, and the token of divine displeasure whereby the Queen, first on horseback, then on foot, is prevented from following the body of her victim. Edward's desire for a fresh resting-place after performing posthumous miracles for twenty years is dated with the same precision in both texts:

Passio 13,8	Eleuatum est itaque sacratissimum corpus eius anno uicesimo primo ex quo illic tumulatum fuerat, qui erat annus ab incarnatione Domini millesimus primus
SEL 251	In þis manere he was issrined. in þe on & twentiþe ȝer Þat þe volk him broȝte fram Waram. & burede him uerst þer A þousond ȝer it was & on. after þulke stonde Þat oure Louerd was an eorþe ibore.

The *Passio* follows this with the *Miracula* but the *SEL* concludes here with a reference to St Edward the Confessor, nephew of the Martyr, and a hope that author and audience may be privileged to join the two saintly and kingly Edwards in heaven.

The editors of the *SEL* draw our attention to certain manuscript variants, but these are not significant in connexion with the relationship to the *Passio*. The longest variant is St Dunstan's prophecy of a disastrous reign for Ethelred, which is non-*Passio* material and is acknowledged to be so by the author, for it comes in the part which he claims to draw from the life of St Alphe.

The Kiplingesque wisdom of another variant links it not with the *Passio* but with the hymn to Edward in a thirteenth-century codex BM Arundel 201 (see below, note 41) and perhaps with *HA:*

SEL 40	For noþing nis fellor þan womman. wanne heo wol to vuel wende
Arundel 201	O feris ferocior furor mulieris
HA	maligne mulieris instinctu.

This brings us to the end of the main versions of the *Passio*. Before we consider what part in the legend was played by the various chronicles to which Dr Wright and Professor Wilson have drawn our attention, it is to be noted that of the material I have so far cited, the only text mentioned by either scholar is the *Dunstanus Saga*. They do not include in their discussion any manuscript of the *Passio* or any manuscript or printed text of the *NLA* or of the breviary lections; nor do they include the edition of Surius, the *Chronicle* of John of Brompton, the collected material of the Bollandists, the translation in the *SEL*, or W. H. Hutton's recent transcription of Sj. And though some of these texts are later than the twelfth-century chroniclers, the *Passio* from which they derive is earlier.

V. CHRONICLES

The chronicles quoted by Dr Wright and Professor Wilson may be divided into three groups: (i) those which are earlier than the *Passio*, (ii) those which are either direct reproduction of the *Passio* or summary of its contents and implications, (iii) those which contain genuine variants from the *Passio*. The three which certainly precede the *Passio* as we now have it are the *Anglo-Saxon Chronicle*, the *Vita Oswaldi* and the reference in *Sermo Lupi*. These do not accuse the stepmother of the murder.

In the second group both the *Dunstanus Saga* and the chronicle of William of Malmesbury contain detailed excerpts from the *Passio*. They include, as well as material on Edward, the *Passio* story of Ethelred's grief for his brother's death which provoked such maternal violence towards him that it left a lifelong impression on his mind.

Osbern and Florence of Worcester perhaps also belong to this group. Osbern's importance is not that he has any detailed information on Edward, but that his *Vita Dunstani* has been thought to contain the first dateable reference to the stepmother's guilt.[27] The way in which Osbern dismisses it in a matter-of-fact manner and a subordinate clause would alone imply that he is mentioning well-known fact, nothing new or disputable. He says simply that Edward having been killed by his stepmother's crime, *novercali fraude occiso*, Ethelred succeeded to the throne. Clearly this version of the story already existed if Osbern can refer so casually to the Queen's part in the murder, and he cannot be responsible for introducing the idea.

A chronicle which neither Dr Wright nor Professor Wilson mentions is of interest and value here, since it is nearly contemporary with Osbern. This is Adam of Bremen's *Gesta Hammaburgensis Ecclesiae Pontificum*.[28] This has in the text the statement that Ethelred was responsible for his brother's death, and has in addition Adam's own marginal correction and expansion that Edgar had a son Edward, *virum sanctissimum*, who was killed by his stepmother in order that she might put her own son on the throne. Adam began his chronicle in 1072 and revised it continually up to his death *c*.1081. His reference may therefore pre-date Osbern's whose *Vita Dunstani* was written before 1093, probably before 1089. More important, Adam's knowledge is obtained from some other source than Osbern's, for Osbern refers to Edward's mother as a veiled virgin seduced by Edgar, whereas Adam is in agreement with the author of the *Passio* that Edward's mother was Edgar's legitimate wife.

Florence of Worcester's sources are apparently three: the *Anglo-Saxon Chronicle* on the murder, the *Vita Oswaldi* on details of the translation to Shaftesbury, and perhaps Osbern for the statement that Edward was killed *jussu nouercae suae Ælfthrythae reginae*. Whether Osbern and Florence obtained their information on Ælfthryth via the *Passio* or indirectly is not evident.

We are left with four chroniclers in group (iii). They are Henry of Huntingdon, John of Wallingford, Walter Map and Gaimar. These need further subdivision. John of Wallingford and Gaimar have long stories containing a mixture of both *Passio* and non-*Passio* material. Henry of Huntingdon and Walter Map have short and slight entries. Henry has the *Anglo-Saxon Chronicle* version, including translation of the poem in the E text, but he tells us also that it is said Edward's stepmother, while she offered him a cup, stabbed him with a small knife (*cultello*). This is the *Passio* version[29] as found in the *Dunstanus Saga*.

In Walter Map's account the drink has become poison, the scene of the crime Shaftesbury. The first error is a confusion of the two points that the Queen offered Edward a drink and that she was responsible for his murder. The second derives from the fact that the body was translated to Shaftesbury, which was the centre of the Edward cult. It seems evident that these particular variants derive from confused memory or inadequate knowledge rather than from discrete tradition.

John of Wallingford and Gaimar on the other hand, have some completely new material. In John of Wallingford's version the stabbing, the concealing of the body and its discovery by divine revelation are *Passio* material, and his title *De Passione Sancti Ædwardi Regis et Martyris* indicates that his sources include hagiography; but the story of the body being wrapped in lead and hidden in the river Stour is not found elsewhere. Similarly in Gaimar the details of the murder, concealment and discovery derive from the *Passio*, but the story is given a setting more appropriate to Middle English romance than to hagiography. The introduction of the dwarf Wolstanet has no parallel in other material.

It is seen that Gaimar and John of Wallingford introduce new details into the story, that Walter Map is confused, that Henry of Huntingdon knows a version which implicates Ælfthryth and one which does not. Nevertheless the bulk of material justifying the existence of "many different stories dealing with the death of Edward" is slight, and the bulk of material showing use, quotation, translation and adaptation of the *Passio* is extensive. And when Dr Wright says that William of Malmesbury is the first to mention Edward's hunting or the Judas kiss, or when he suggests that "a change is perhaps to be noted in the treatment of the king's character" he is drawing erroneous conclusions. These details concern material which his chroniclers derive from a single source, the *Passio*. There is little justification for assumptions about lost literature, and little evidence for the multi-development of legends.

VI. SOURCES OF THE PASSIO

The author of the *Passio* claims to use nothing that he has not found in writing or heard on reliable testimony. His fullest reference to his methods is at 11,22-26. Here he points out that many miracles took place at Edward's shrine for which no written record survives. These he omits "quam de sancto uiro alia quam quae fideliter scripta repperimus, aut quae fidelium relatione didicimus, inconsiderate diceremus." At 13,15 and at 15,20 he refers again to the extent of the material he has rejected because he has not found it adequately documented.

At 14,12 and 14,19 he claims reliable oral testimony as his source, and at 15,8 he defines what he means by reliable: "ii quibus sanior mens inerat, nequaquam facile ad credendum persuaderi poterant."

The *Miracula* are in fact only three in number, since all miracles which occurred before 1001 are included in the *Passio*. Two of these three are the ones for which the author claims oral testimony as his source, which implies that the written sources to which he refers are sources for the *Passio* itself.

On comparing the *Passio* with the earliest texts on Edward, we find that some of the material is the same. Nothing in the *Anglo-Saxon Chronicle*'s brief statement is at variance with the *Passio* account. The *Vita Oswaldi* has some details which the *Passio* echoes, such as Edward's visit to Corfe being motivated by affection for his brother Ethelred:

Passio 4,15   eum puro et sincero corde diligebat
Vita Oswaldi   desiderans consolationem fraterni amoris.

Other details are not shared. The *Passio* does not give Edward's actual words to his murderer, and where the *Vita* tells us that Bishop Sidemann was Edward's tutor, in the *Passio* the better-known Dunstan has this role. More significantly, the *Passio* has no verbal echoes of the *Vita* even where its material is the same. It is improbable that the author of the *Passio* made use of it.

Accounts of Edward's coronation are very much alike in the *Vitae Dunstani*[30] of Osbern and Eadmer and in the *Passio*. It is not clear that any one of these is a source for the others, and the most probable explanation of the similarity may be a common source for all three:

Passio 2,19   uexillum crucis sanctae, quod ex consuetudine prae se ferebatur, arreptum in medio statuit, eumque . . . in regem consecrauit
Osbern p.114   Dunstanus arrepto crucis vexillo, quod prae se ex more ferebatur, in medio constitit, Edwardum illis ostendit, elegit, sacravit . . .
Eadmer p.214   Dunstanus . . . arrepto sanctae Crucis vexillo, medius constitit et . . . Edwardum regem constituit . . .

One source which the *Passio* undoubtedly uses for historical material on Edgar is the *Regularis Concordia*.[31] There are differences of fact between the two in that they posit different wives for Edgar, but it is obviously in the *Passio*'s interest that the benevolent activities of Edgar's queen shall be attributed to Edward's mother, not his stepmother. Some of the vocabulary is copied almost without change:

Passio 1,23   ut uidelicet mas maribus et femina feminis absque ulla suspicione conuenientius subueniret.
R.C. 3   ut uidelicet mas maribus, femina feminis sine ullo suspicionis scrupulo subueniret.

That the traditions of Shaftesbury itself were a major source for the *Passio* is indicated by the presence of parallel material in the *Passio* and the Shaftesbury cartulary.[32] The author of the *Passio* knows, and digresses in order to mention, that the convent was founded there by Alfred who made his daughter abbess. And the *Passio*, so far as I know, is the only text which mentions specifically that Alfred's gifts to Shaftesbury included a hundred hides of land, apart from the charter itself which records the gift.

Another charter, this time confirming the *Passio*'s account of the events of 1001[33] is also preserved in the Shaftesbury cartulary. According to the *Passio*, Edward, twenty-one years after his translation, appeared in visions and sent messages to his brother Ethelred, demanding to be moved to a different resting-place. A charter of 1001 contains Ethelred's grant of Bradford-on-Avon to Shaftesbury so that the relics of Edward might be kept there during the time of enemy invasions. Among the names witnessing the charter are Wulfsige of Sherborne, and the name and title *Ælfsige abbas*, which occurs twice. These two are the abbots of Ely and of New Minster, Winchester. The *Passio* connects with the event the name of Wulfsige of Sherborne, but is vague about a certain *praesul* of great sanctity called Elfsinus. Such an indeterminate reference indicates that Shaftesbury tradition venerated the name, but the author of the *Passio* could not attach an identity to it. Probably the Elfsinus who was remembered was the Winchester abbot, who very likely interested himself in the Edward cult, since some of the earliest indications of it are in the liturgical books of New Minster. Such an interest would account for his being warmly remembered at Shaftesbury; and if he was instrumental in the development of the cult, this would account for the Winchester emphasis.

Evidence for the *Passio*'s sources is very meagre, but it does allow us to draw certain conclusions. One is that it is only in the early paragraphs on historical background that the *Passio* has any resemblance to other post-Conquest writings, and only here that a specific source, the *Regularis Concordia*, can be traced. Secondly, the author divides his sources into oral and written and gives us the details of his oral sources. This implies written source elsewhere, and this division is corroborated by the time-gap involved. The *Passio* stops at 1001, the first of the *Miracula* is reported from the time of Edward the Confessor, the second is *nec multo post*, the third involves Hermann, Bishop of Salisbury. Hermann did not become bishop of Salisbury till the see was transferred there in 1075, though of course the miracle could have taken place earlier. We have silence on Edward, in fact, until we come to the miracles which occurred within the lifetime of those who reported them to the author. In the case of John of Vermand who came to find healing at Edward's tomb in the days of the Confessor, the author says that he spent the rest of his life serving in the monastery, as those still there who saw him can testify. In the case of the other cure involving Hermann, the author says he has heard of it from those who saw it take place.

Both those who remember when John of Vermand was at Shaftesbury, and those who witnessed the later cure, are obviously Shaftesbury inhabitants, and it is evident from the comparison with the cartulary and with the oral testimony that Shaftesbury nuns told the author of the *Passio* details of their history, and probably turned over their documents to him for consultation. It is to be expected further that Shaftesbury abbey would have provided itself with a life of Edward fairly early; the lack of information on miracles immediately after 1001 suggests that such a life was composed shortly after the events of that year.

The author of the *Passio* in its extant form claims to be re-writing what he has found written. I suggest that what he found was a life of St Edward from accession to final resting-place, to which he added historical material on Edgar at the beginning, and recent miracles at the end, and which he expanded with other details of information. The detail about the castle at Corfe which was not there in Edward's reign is clearly a post-Conquest addition, since Corfe belonged to the first phase of Norman castle-building. The account of the hundred hides of land (*hidas*) is perhaps another of his interpolations, since the Latinization of vernacular words is a post-Conquest rather than a pre-Conquest habit. The material on St Edith might also be an insertion.

VII. AUTHOR OF THE PASSIO

If we accept the personal testimony of the author on the two late miracles, he must have been writing in the last quarter of the eleventh century or the first few years of the twelfth. Hardy suggests that he may have been Eadmer who wrote a hymn to Edward. But at least one other hagiographer shares this distinction, for Goscelin who wrote the life of St Edith included in his work a poem to her martyred brother.

There is, I think, no very positive evidence for attributing the *Passio* to any known hagiographer, but such evidence as we have points to Goscelin. He is writing at about the right date, and his interest centres on Anglo-Saxon saints. He writes the life of St Edith, Edward's sister, and obviously has close connexions with Sherborne and Wilton, the Dorset area where the Edward story was localized. An account of Goscelin by C. H. Talbot[34] demonstrates that it was Goscelin's habit to collect material for his biographies on the spot where the saint was venerated, which accords also with what we know of the author of the *Passio*. More significant perhaps is the mention of Hermann of Salisbury and the author's attitude towards him. Hermann was Goscelin's patron and Goscelin deeply admired him. The author of the *Passio* describes him as *uenerabilis* and reports him as a major agent in one of Edward's cures.

Two of the manuscripts of the *Passio* include it next to Goscelin's work, Sj before Goscelin on St Augustine, C between Goscelin on the Barking saints and Goscelin on Edith. Talbot includes the *Passio* with a query in his list of Goscelin's works. The *Passio* does not contain the words which Talbot cites as particularly characteristic of Goscelin's vocabulary, but in syntax and style the *Passio* seems to me to resemble Goscelin's work more closely than that of the hagiographers Osbern and Eadmer.

If the work is Goscelin's, it seems probable that it was written during the same decade as the rest of his work on the saints of the Midlands and Western England, i.e. 1070–1080, since in the following decade he settled at Canterbury and worked on the Canterbury saints.

VIII. DEVELOPMENT OF THE CULT OF ST EDWARD

That the *Passio* as we have it is a re-writing of an earlier life is the author's own statement, but reason alone would suggest that a saint who was so deeply venerated so soon after his death would not have to wait half a century for the writing of his *Passio*. And the evidence for the early establishment of an Edward cult is considerable. Even in the *Anglo-Saxon Chronicle* (E text) Edward is described as a *heofonlic sanct*, and the poem on him says that though his killers wished to eliminate all memory of him (cf. *Passio* 7,8), God has spread his fame in heaven and earth, and those who would not do him honour in life now pay honour to his bones. Whatever doubts there are about the date of composition of *Chronicle* entries, the wording of the poem suggests that it was composed during the lifetime of Edward's enemies. I am not clear what the poet means by God having avenged Edward though his kin would not. The *Vita Oswaldi* has a reference to the blindness divinely inflicted on one of the murderers, but it may be that the poet, Wulfstan-like, was thinking rather of enemy raids as God's punishment of Ethelred and the English. The statements of the poem are rhetorical, but the poet has a precise knowledge of the situation which suggests he is not too far distanced from it. It would be interesting to know what date one could put on the 980 entry concerning the translation of the body to Shaftesbury, and whether the word "holy" used of Edward is part of the original text. It is worth noting in this context that the Abingdon manuscript of the *Chronicle*, the C text, though it does not have the poem on Edward, uses the word *gemartyrad* where the E text and others have the neutral verb *ofslegen*.

The charter of 1001 already mentioned describes Edward as saint and martyr, and the words are also used in contemporary literature. Adelard's *Vita Dunstani* for example has a casual reference to *sanctum Eadwardum martyrem*. The *Vita Oswaldi* account of Edward is important too, not for its negative evidence on Ælfthryth, but because it demonstrates the veneration early accorded to Edward. It is indeed a miniature hagiography in itself, complete with accounts of the martyr's welcome into heaven and his posthumous miracles, to one of which the author cites archbishop Ælfric as witness. Fisher, though putting the *Vita Oswaldi* later than most scholars have done, still calls it certainly pre-Conquest (see below, note 3) but the reference to Ælfric in present not past tense suggests a date before his death in 1005: "Est huius rei testis Ælfricus archiepiscopus civitatis Cantiae." That there is nothing about the 1001 ceremony, though much about posthumous miracles, and divine vengeance, may perhaps indicate a date of composition before that ceremony had taken place. If it were written while Ælfthryth was still alive and influential, this would after all be an excellent reason for not connecting her name with the murder. But whichever date one prefers, the *Vita Oswaldi* is a powerful piece of pre-Conquest evidence for the popularity of the martyred Edward. The extent to which the technicalities of hagiographical language colour the text which is commonly considered our primary source is also worth noting.

In 1008, during Ethelred's reign, Edward's mass day was ordered to be observed throughout England: "7 *sancte* Eadwerdes mæssedæg witan habbað gecoren, þaet man freolsian sceal ofer eal Englaland on XV kl. Aprilis."[35] Such an order presumably regularizes an existing situation; Shaftesbury and New Minster Winchester were no doubt already celebrating the feast.

In *English Kalendars before 1100*[36] Professor Wormald prints nineteen such calendars, and a study of these shows that Edward's day was being widely celebrated from an early date. Only two of the calendars, one of which is ninth-century, do not have an entry for Edward. A further two which are tenth-century have Edward added on the appropriate day in a later hand. Two others have Edward expunged. One of these is the Bosworth Psalter into which Edward was inserted and from which he was erased, apparently within the first few years of the eleventh century. It must have been a controversial entry. But this leaves us with thirteen pre-1100 calendars in which March 18th is St Edward's day. In seven of these the entry is in capitals, placing it among the important festivals; in five, as well as the March entry there is one for Edward's translation on February 13th.

Professor Wormald dates to the first half of the century four calendars which contain Edward. One from Christ Church Canterbury he dates 1012-23, and this is one in which Edward's feast is in capitals. Two are from New Minster Winchester (Hyde Abbey), in one of which *c*.1025 Edward's translation is also celebrated, while in the other his feast appears as *Passio sancti Eadwardi regis et martyris*. This is unusual, occurring in only one other calendar, a mid-century one from Bury St Edmund's. To the Winchester calendar Professor Wormald assigns a date between 1023 and 1035, and it is significant that the term *Passio* was in use as early as this. The fourth early calendar is from Worcester, from the second quarter of the century, and here again Edward's feast is in capitals.

Another three of the thirteen calendars are pre-Conquest. Two of them, the Bury St Edmund's one with the entry *Passio*, and one from Sherborne in the locality of the Edward cult, celebrate also his translation in February.

The calendar in the Missal of Robert of Jumièges[37] appears to be the earliest that includes Edward. The editor assigns the missal to a date between 1008 and 1025, suggesting one between 1013 and 1017. He points out that the festivals of the highest rank are marked by gold uncial characters, and specifies Edward's as one of these.

There are "five fairly complete mass-books of probable English provenance remaining from before 1100."[38] Two of these, the Leofric Missal and the Winchcombe sacramentary, are tenth-century and irrelevant. The other three all contain masses for Edward's day. They are:

    (i) The Missal of Robert of Jumièges;
    (ii) BM Cotton Vitellius A XVIII;
    (iii) Le Havre, Bibliothèque Municipale 330.[39]

The Robert Missal is the earliest of these and contains two masses for Edward, not in their place in the *Proprium*, but on the opening leaves, together with the masses for saints Guthlac, Botolph, Alban and Kenelm. Le Havre 330, which is from Winchester, is assigned by its editor to the second half of the eleventh century, and contains one mass for Edward. This is a different one from either of the two in Robert's Missal. The second of these two, however, is found also in Cotton Vitellius, a sacramentary written at Wells between 1061 and 1088.

The Missal of Robert of Jumièges is assigned by its editor to Winchester, but Neil Ker rejects this ascription. This leaves us with three possible forms of the mass for Edward's day from the eleventh century. One of these, Le Havre, is the New Minster Winchester form, another is found in two unrelated manuscripts and may well be the Shaftesbury form, since it is the one which ultimately finds its way into the Salisbury breviary.

Prayers to Edward occur in other eleventh-century service-books. BM Arundel 155 a Psalter from Christ Church Canterbury, written between 1012 and 1023, includes Edward in a corporate prayer to the martyrs. Only a small number of martyrs are invoked, but two of the seven, Edward and Ælfheah, are local saints. The Cambridge MS Corpus Christi 391, the *Portiforium Oswaldi* from Worcester, written in the second half of the century, contains a prayer *In Natale Sc̄i Eaduuardi Regis* identical with the opening prayer in the first mass of Robert's Missal. BM Additional 28,188, a Benedictional from Exeter, from the second quarter of the century, contains three prayers to Edward, a group with no verbal resemblances to the prayers in any other manuscript.

None of the prayers contains much information, but the one in Robert's Missal (found again in MS Corpus Christi 391) refers both to the manner of Edward's death and to the miracles already occurring: "Deus qui beatum eaduueardum regem anglorum iniustae occisum piae iustificas et miris signis mundanis declaras . . ." A prayer in Additional hopes for help against enemy raids in words that recall the *Passio* lament:

Add. 28,188   ab omni inimicorum incursu nos ipso intercedente custodiat
f.277r

Passio 7,31   Quis nos ab hostium incursionibus . . . liberabit.

This of course suggests not textual relationship but the fact that people had enemy raids much on their minds.

Edward's name also appears frequently in eleventh-century litanies. Some of these occur in the service-books already mentioned, but there are others in Pontificals, Psalters, and miscellaneous collections of devotional material. The litanies in which I have noted Edward among the martyrs are those in:

(i) BM Additional 28,188.
(ii) BM Arundel 60, a Winchester New Minster Psalter, c.1060.
(iii) BM Cotton Titus D XXVI, a miscellany from Winchester New Minster, eleventh century.
(iv) BM Cotton Tiberius A III, from Christ Church Canterbury, mid-century.
(v) BM Cotton Vitellius A VII, a Pontifical (?Ramsey) second quarter of the century.
(vi) BM Harley 863, a Psalter from Exeter, third quarter of the century.
(vii) Bodleian Douce 296, a Psalter (?Crowland) mid-century.
(viii) Bodleian Laud 482, Worcester, mid-century.
(ix) Cambridge, Corpus Christi 391, the *Portiforium Oswaldi*, second half of the century.
(x) Cambridge, Corpus Christi 422, the "Red Book of Darley", mid-century.
(xi) Cambridge, Corpus Christi 44, a Pontifical probably from St. Augustine's Canterbury, eleventh-century, with two litanies

which include Edward.

(xii) Bibliothèque Nationale Fonds Latin 8824, the Paris Psalter, mid-century.

Professor Wormald, in his discussion of the litany containing Edward in Arundel 60,[40] suggests that it was copied almost without alteration from one composed at Winchester between 988 and 1012. In addition to the eleventh-century service-books there are two twelfth-century Psalters which, though late, are of interest because they originate from Shaftesbury, and show the extent to which Edward's cult flourished there. In BM Cotton Nero C IV there are no fewer than four calendar entries for Edward King and Martyr: two February ones for his *aduentus* and *translatio*, a March one for his *passio* and a June one for his *festiuitas*. BM Lansdowne 383 has only one calendar entry, though a red-letter one, for Edward, but in the litany he comes straight after Stephen the protomartyr, honoured by capitals though Stephen and Edmund on either side of him are not, and again in the prayer for the intercession of all martyrs, his name is specified and specialized in capitals.

Hymns to Edward occur spasmodically and in less predictable places than litanies and calendars do. In looking at these I have not restricted myself to the century after Edward's death, though some of them were certainly written in that century. The poem on Edward in the *Anglo-Saxon Chronicle* may be the earliest and is the only one in the vernacular. But one very early one is the poem on the translation of Edward written on a blank leaf in an eleventh-century manuscript, BM Harley 1117, which is otherwise centred on St Cuthbert. This has not to my knowledge been printed and I append it below.

The *Analecta Hymnica*[41] prints hymns to Edward from two manuscripts: a fifteen-stanza one, antagonistic towards women and stepmothers, found in BM Arundel 201, a manuscript which Neil Ker dates to the late twelfth or early thirteenth century, and ascribes tentatively to Wymondham, Norfolk, originally a priory and cell of St. Albans, Hertfordshire; and two short ones from MS Col. 28, a fifteenth-century manuscript which apparently contains a further hymn in prose which the editors have not included. The attitude of these hymns is enthusiastic and the vocabulary ritualistic:

O Edwarde flos martyrum
Velut rosa vel lilium,

but since exactly the same hymn is given for Edmund with change of name only, it is not a significant addition to the evidence for Edward's cult.

The *Repertorium Hymnologicum*[42] refers to the hymns in *Analecta Hymnica* and also to one in Cambridge MS Peterhouse 94, which is actually a hymn to a later Edward, not to the martyr. The *Repertorium* does not include the hymns of either Goscelin or Eadmer. Goscelin's occurs in his life of St Edith, and is printed in the edition of that life.[43] It is certainly earlier than 1089, since the life is dedicated to Lanfranc who died in that year. Like the other hymns it is laudatory rather than informative. Three hymns by Eadmer which have apparently not been printed are transcribed below. They are found in the Cambridge manuscript Corpus Christi 371, a manuscript from Christ Church Canterbury containing the works of Eadmer. The hymns must have been composed before the year 1124 in which Eadmer died.

The evidence suggests that Edward had a mass for his day, his name in the litany and his feast in the calendar well within the first quarter of the eleventh century, and very soon after the Witan's order to this effect. It suggests further that his cult, begun no doubt at Shaftesbury, was early established at Winchester and Canterbury, and flourished throughout the century and throughout the south of England. It is unlikely that, given this degree of enthusiasm and interest, there should be an interval of another fifty years before the writing of his *Passio*. I suggest that the *Passio* as we have it, is a re-writing of an early Shaftesbury life, with added introduction, interpolations and *Miracula*. Such a conclusion is speculative. But whatever the date of the *Passio* in its original form, it is necessary to remember that the chroniclers themselves had no hesitation in drawing on hagiography. The author of the *Passio* first or second redaction, may be an unreliable historian, adding little to our knowledge of actual events, but the *Passio* is a primary source, and it is on the *Passio* that the Edward cult is based, and from the *Passio* that almost all writing on Edward derives.[44]

In addition to the prayers, the litanies, the hymns and the lections, the *Passio* as it stands in two basic manuscripts, Dy and R, is itself demonstrably for liturgical use. Since we are frequently reminded that education was in the hands of the monasteries, we might perhaps consider how many times during his education the average chronicler would have sat through the celebrations of Edward's feast day. Such an exercise will at least take us away from speculation about popular imaginings and oral sagas, and remind us of the extent to which we are dealing with liturgical rather than literary material.

---

[1] C. E. Wright, *The Cultivation of Saga in Anglo-Saxon England* (Edinburgh & London, 1939), pp. 161-71.

[2] J. Earle and C. Plummer, *Two of the Saxon Chronicles Parallel* (Oxford, 1892), pp. 122-23.

[3] Ed. J. Raine, *The Historians of the Church of York and its Archbishops* (Rolls Series 71, 1879-86), Vol. 1, pp. 448-52. The *Vita Oswaldi*, if one accepts Dr. Wright's dating to 1008, is thirty years after the murder, not thirteen as he claims; but see D. J. V. Fisher "The Anti-Monastic Reaction in the Reign of Edward the Martyr," *Cambridge Historical Journal*, 10 (1952), pp. 254-92.

[4] R. M. Wilson, *The Lost Literature of Medieval England* (London, 1952), pp. 111-13; 2nd ed. (London, 1970), pp. 101-03.

5   Florence of Worcester, *Chronicon ex Chronicis*, ed. B. Thorpe (English Historical Society, 1848), Vol. 1, p. 145.
    Henry of Huntingdon, *Historia Anglorum*, ed. T. Arnold (Rolls Series 74, 1879), p. 167.
    William of Malmesbury, *De Regum Gestis Anglorum*, ed. W. Stubbs (Rolls Series 90, 1887), Vol. 1, p. 183.
    Walter Map, *De Nugis Curialium*, ed. M. R. James (Anecdota Oxoniensa: Medieval and Modern Series, Vol. 14, 1914), p. 207.
    Gaimar, *Lestorie des Engles*, ed. T. D. Hardy and C. T. Martin (Rolls Series 91, 1888), pp. 168-73.
    John of Wallingford, *Chronica*, ed. R. Vaughan (Royal Historical Society, Camden Third Series 90, Camden Miscellany Vol. 21, 1958), pp. 56-57.
    Osbern, *Vita Sancti Dunstani*, ed. W. Stubbs, *Memorials of St. Dunstan* (Rolls Series 63, 1874), p. 114.
    Wulfstan, *Sermo Lupi ad Anglos*, ed. D. Whitelock (London 1939, 3rd ed. 1963), p. 56.
    Dunstanus Saga, ed. C. E. Fell (Editiones Arnamagnæanæ, Copenhagen, 1963), pp. xlviii-liv, 10-11.
6   *Bibliotheca Hagiographica Latina*, ed. Socii Bollandiani (Brussels, 1898-1899, reprinted 1949), p. 363.
7   T. D. Hardy, *Descriptive Catalogue of Materials Relating to the History of Great Britain and Ireland* (Rolls Series 26, 1862-71), Vol. 1, Part 2, pp. 579-82.
8   Surius, *De Probatis Sanctorum Historiis* (Cologne, 1571), Vol. 2, pp. 276-79.
    Acta Sanctorum, ed. J. Bollandus et al. (Paris & Rome, 1865) March 2, pp. 637-46.
9   Ed. C. Horstman, *Nova Legenda Anglie* (Oxford, 1901), pp. 349-51.
10 John of Brompton, *Chronicon*, ed. R. Twysden *Historiae Anglicanae Scriptores X* (1652), columns 872-76. MSS: Cambridge, Corpus Christi 96 (*JB CC*); BM Cotton Tiberius C XIII (*JB BM*).
11 Petrus de Natalibus, *Catalogus Sanctorum et gestorum eorum* (Venice, 1506), pp. 208-09.
12 My thanks are due to Mr R. W. Hunt of the Bodleian library for this information, and for his expert examination of Rawlinson C 440 and Digby 146.
13 *Op. cit.*, p. xv.
14 *Catalogue*, Vol. 1, Part 2, p. 640.
15 *Les manuscrits de la Reine de Suède au Vatican. Réédition du catalogue de Montfaucon et cotes actuelles*, Studi e Testi (Vatican City, 1964), p. 72.
16 *The South English Legendary*, ed. C. d'Evelyn and A. J. Mill (EETS, 1956), Vol. 1, pp. 110-18.
17 For the dating and provenance of these manuscripts I have relied on N. R. Ker's *Medieval Libraries of Great Britain* (Royal Historical Society, 2nd ed., 1964).
18 M. L. Colker "Texts of Jocelyn of Canterbury which relate to the history of Barking Abbey," *Studia Monastica*, 7 (1965), p. 394.
19 *Chronicon Monasterii de Abingdon*, ed. J. Stevenson (Rolls Series 2, 1858), Vol. 1, p. 443: "Tempore etiam Cnutonis regis reliquiae Sancti Eadwardi, regis et martyris, quae in ista continentur ecclesia, ad hanc domum Abbendonensem mirifice sunt delatae; prout in serie passionis et vitae gloriosissimi martyris evidentissime continetur." The clause referring to the *Passio* occurs only in the later of the two manuscripts of the *Chronicon*, the late thirteenth-century BM Cotton Claudius B VI.
20 F. Jacobs and F. A. Ukert, *Beiträge zur ältern Litteratur oder Merkwürdigkeiten der Herzoglichen Öffentlichen Bibliothek zu Gotha*, Vol. 3, Part 2 (Leipzig 1843), pp. 271 ff.
    M. L. Colker, "A Gotha Codex Dealing with the Saints of Barking Abbey," *Studia Monastica*, 10 (1968), p. 321.
21 In the *Annales de Wintonia* attributed to Richard of Devizes the horse galloped "ad locum qui dicitur Edwardestowe" and left the blood-stained saddle there. Edwardstow is a common name for Shaftesbury, as can be seen from Domesday Book references. These annals are edited by H. R. Luard in *Annales Monastici* (Rolls Series 36, 1865), Vol. 2 p. 13.
22 This prayer occurs in the early eleventh-century Missal of Robert of Jumièges; see below, note 37. The mass containing it is the one which Sarum adopts.

23 The text of the *Nova Legenda Anglie* is related to *JB*, though not taken from it directly. Also related to *JB* are the fifteenth-century redactions of the *Passio* in martyrologies; see, for example, B. de Gaiffier "Le Martyrologe et le legendier d'Hermann Greven," *Analecta Bollandiana*, 54 (1936), pp. 316-58. *JB* itself exists in two manuscripts which link with different groups of *Passio* manuscripts, notably at 2,21. There is scope for much work on these later texts and their relationships both with the *Passio* and with each other, and especially there is a need for work on John of Brompton.
24 The brief description of this manuscript in the Cotton catalogue notes only that it is a lectionary and thirteenth-century. I have not found any information on it elsewhere. An inscription in a blank space on f.30r says that it is *liber Roberti Taylor de wick curatoris in chomit. Wigor. 1623.*
25 W. H. Hutton *The English Saints* (Bampton Lectures, 1903), pp. 155-80.
26 Perhaps Caversham because of its closeness to Reading which claimed relics of Edward. Mr D. A. Bethall of University College, Dublin, has kindly given me information on Edward's relics.
27 See, for example, F. M. Stenton, *Anglo-Saxon England*, 2nd ed. (Oxford, 1947), p. 368.
28 W. Trillmich and R. Buchner, *Quellen des 9. und 11. Jahrhunderts zur Geschichte der hamburgischen Kirche und des Reiches* (Darmstadt, 1961), p. 292. It is possible that information reached Adam of Bremen via Scandinavia. Cnut seems to have been pro-Edward, which may have been useful for him politically. He restated Ethelred's law on the observance of Edward's feast-day and concerned himself in the distribution of Edward's relics. That a text of the *Passio* reached Iceland is a further indication of Scandinavian interest in Edward.
29 The existence of two versions — one in which the Queen arranged the murder, and another in which she committed it — may be partially due to manuscript marginalia. For example in the Cambridge manuscript of Symeon of Durham, Corpus Christ 139, f.35r, the text has *iussu nouercae suae* but a marginal heading simplifies this to *Eaduuardus rex anglorum a nouerca sua occisus est*.
30 Stubbs, *Memorials of St. Dunstan*.
31 *Regularis Concordia*, ed. T. Symons (Nelson's Medieval Classics, 1953), ch. 3, p. 2.
32 MS BM Harley 61; see P. H. Sawyer, *Anglo-Saxon Charters* (Royal Historical Society, 1968), Nos. 357 and 899. Comment on the Alfred charter suggests it is unlikely to be authentic, but clearly it contains a genuine Shaftesbury tradition and claim. The land specified in the charter is recorded as Shaftesbury property in Domesday Book. Mrs Stafford who is working on the Ethelred charters assures me that Sawyer 899 can be accepted as genuine.
33 There are some interesting dates here. The translation to Shaftesbury is in all sources linked with Ælfhere of Mercia who dies shortly afterwards. Then there is silence on Edward during Ælfthryth's lifetime. She died after 998 and before 1002. It seems likely that the 1001 ceremony and charter were the result of popular pro-Edward feeling or episcopal pressure as soon as Ælfthryth's power was removed. There is evidence that she continued to be a dominant influence on Ethelred and presumably on the kingdom so long as she lived. It is worth noting also that the Chronicle of Æthelweard (ed. A. Campbell, Medieval Texts, London 1962) has a chapter heading *De regimine Eaduuerdi regis et de nece ipsius*. This chapter is not written, the Chronicle ending with the death of Edgar. Professor Campbell suggests that this may be because Æthelweard's source did not provide any matter after the death of Edgar, but it is at least equally probable that his failure to complete the work according to his intentions was a matter of diplomacy. He died about the same time as Ælfthryth, c. 998.
34 C. H. Talbot, "The Liber confortarius of Goscelin of Saint Bertin," *Analecta Monastica* Series 3 (1955), p. 13.
35 F. Liebermann, *Die Gesetze der Angelsachsen* (Halle, 1903, reprinted Leipzig, 1935), pp. 240-41, V Æthelred 16. The exact wording is used again in Cnut's Laws, pp. 298-99 I Cnut 17,1.
36 F. Wormald, *English Kalendars Before A.D. 1100* (Henry Bradshaw Society 72, 1934).
37 *The Missal of Robert of Jumièges*, ed. H. A. Wilson (Henry Bradshaw Society 11, 1896)

38 *The Missal of the New Minster Winchester*, ed. D. H. Turner (Henry Bradshaw Society 93, 1962), p. vi.
39 See note 38.
40 F. Wormald "The English Saints in the Litany in Arundel MS. 60" *Analecta Bollandiana* 64 (1946), pp. 72-86. I have relied on Professor Wormald's contribution to the Preface to *The Paris Psalter*, ed. Bertram Colgrave ch. 6 note 73, and on N. R. Ker's *Medieval Libraries* for provenance and dating of most of these liturgical manuscripts. The material is touched on briefly in B. Fehr's "Altenglische Ritualtexte für Krankenbesuch, heilige Ölung und Begrabnis" *Texte und Forschungen zur Englischen Kulturgeschichte*. Festgabe für Felix Liebermann (Halle, 1921) p. 38.
41 *Analecta Hymnica Medii Ævi*, ed. C. Blume and G. M. Dreves (Leipzig, 1898), Vol. 28, p. 292, Vol. 29, pp. 72-74.
42 *Repertorium Hymnologicum*, ed. U. Chevalier (Louvain, 1892-1920).
43 A Wilmart "La légende de Ste Édith en prose et vers par le moine Goscelin," *Analecta Bollandiana*, 56 (1938), pp. 83-84.
44 The one tradition which really stands out as distinct from the *Passio* is Wulfstan's statement that Edward's body was burned, information which not only is not given elsewhere, but which directly contradicts *Anglo-Saxon Chronicle*, *Vita Oswaldi* and *Passio* statements about the translation of the body. *Forbærned* implies utterly destroyed by burning, and it is perhaps a word that throws light on *Chronicle* and *Passio* report that Edward's murderers tried to eliminate all memory of him from the earth. A cult of course needs relics, which may be why no other source mentions burning.

MANUSCRIPTS

A   BM Additional 11,881

C   Cardiff Public Library 1.381

Db   Trinity College Dublin 171

Dy   Bodleian Digby 146

G   Gotha Landesbibliothek Memb. I 81

Lb   Lambeth Palace Library 149

Ln   BM Lansdowne 436

R   Bodleian Rawlinson C 440

Sj   St John's Oxford 96

39r INCIPIT PASSIO SANCTI EADWARDI REGIS ET MARTYRIS

Inclitus rex Eadwardus alto et nobilissimo regum antiquorum stemmate in Brittannia oriundus fuit, quodque his maius est ab ipso pueritiae suae flore, a sancto Dunstano Cantuariensi archipraesule Christi regeneratus sacramentis, morum honestate coepit pollere.
 Extitit autem piae memoriae rege, Edgaro nomine, progenitus, qui inter cunctos Brittanniae reges tam in procinctu bellorum quam in Dei rebus uelut lucifer radiis probitatis suae effulserat; nam postquam monarchiam regni Deo fauente prudenter adeptus est, omnes insulas totius regionis, in quibus ante eum diuersi reges principabantur, suo imperio adauxit. Dein etiam hortantibus et docentibus praedicto archipraesule, et sancto Æthelwoldo Wintoniensi episcopo, multa suae patriae destituta ac exinanita monasteria de suo fecit restaurari, nonnulla uero a fundamentis aedificari. Abbates quoque cum monachorum turbis sub disciplinae iugo regulariter uicturos in quibusdam dirigit, in quibusdam autem sanctimonialium congregationes statuit feminarum, conferens praedia ac uillas ad uictum et uestitum eorum sufficienter. Taliter itaque rebus in domo Dei dispositis, studens gloriosus rex ut fieret sanctae matri ecclesiae munimento exterius et ornamento interius, inter cetera probitatum suarum insignia hoc ab eo decretum est, ut de monachis in congregatione positis ipse tanquam pastor prouidus eos, frequenter uisitando et consolando curam gereret: et uxor eius sanctimonialium conuenticula tanquam mater piissima procuraret, ut uidelicet mas maribus et femina feminis absque ulla suspicione conuenientius subueniret.

39v
 Habebat / etiam idem praeclarus rex ex alia coniuge nomine

  Incipit *to* martyris, A Db R *add* quintodecimo kalendas aprilis, C Vita beati Ædwardi Regis et Martyris, Lb Incipit uita sancti edwardi regis et martiris, Ln Incipit de sancto eadwardo anglorum rege et martire glorioso.
1 Inclitus, G *begins here*
2 his, G R id
4 honestate coepit, C G Lb Ln R *transpose*
7 Dei rebus, Lb ecclesiasticis rebus disponendis
7 nam *to* subueniret (24), Ln *omits*
10 Dein *to* subueniret (24), G *omits*
10 etiam, R *omits*
11 Æthelwoldo Wintoniensi, Db oswaldo wigornensi
18 sanctae, Db R sancti
18 munimento, R in munimento
19 probitatum, Db probatum
23 mas maribus *to* sic posse (7,3), *lacuna in* A
25 rex, G *adds* Eadgarus

Ælftrid filium alterum, cui nomen erat Æthelredus. Sed praedictus filius suus bonae indolis adolescens Eadwardus nequaquam lasciuiae aut uoluptatibus illecebrosae carnis mentem intendit; sed talem se in omnibus exhibere studuit, ut Deo super omnia in integritate mentis et corporis complaceret, et ab hominibus pio diligeretur affectu. Videns uero pater eius tantam in filio carissimo animi florere ingenuitatem, gauisus super prudentia eius et industria, hunc post se in solio iure hereditario inthronizandum paterno more instituit ac praeordinauit. Interea compositis et subactis, ut praemisimus, in pace et tranquillitate totius regni partibus, memoratus rex piissimus Edgarus ex hac subtractus est uita a domino, ut credimus, gaudia percepturus aeterna, anno dominicae incarnationis nongentesimo quinquagesimo uicesimo septimo, principatus autem sui anno sextodecimo, mense Iulio, die octauo mensis eiusdem.

Quo mortuo, filius eius senior Eadwardus ex uoluntate patris, ut praelibauimus, a sancto Dunstano et quibusdam principibus ad regni gubernacula suscipienda eligitur. Sed dum consecrationis eius tempore nonnulli patriae optimates resistere uoluissent, sanctus Dunstanus in electione eius unanimiter perseuerans, uexillum crucis sanctae, quod ex consuetudine prae se ferebatur, arreptum in medio statuit, eumque cum reliquis religiosis episcopis in regem consecrauit, quem etiam paterno affectu toto quo aduixit tempore dilexit, quia eum ab annis puerilibus sibi in filium adoptauerat.

2   suus, G *omits*
3   mentem, C mente
4   in integritate, G Lb R *omit* in
5   corporis, Lb *adds* et in ceteris pietatis operibus
5   hominibus, Db G Lb omnibus
5   diligeretur affectu, Lb *transposes*
7   gauisus, Ln *adds* est
7   prudentia eius, Lb *transposes*
8   solio, Lb R *add* regni
9   Interea, Lb Igitur
9   Interea *to* adoptauerat (23), Ln *omits*
10   tranquillitate, Lb *adds* circumquaque
10   rex, Lb *adds* edgarus cursu uite in senectute bona consumpto non sine graui luctu
12   anno, Lb *adds* uidelicet
13   quinquagesimo uicesimo, Lb septuagesimo
13   sui, G *omits*
14   Iulio, Lb iulii
15   Quo mortuo, Dy *begins here* (M)ortuo edgaro rege (*NLA also begins here*)
15   senior, Lb *omits*
15-16   ut praelibauimus, Dy *omits*
17   Sed dum, G Necdum
18   patriae, Lb *omits*
19   crucis sanctae, Db G Lb R (*JB*) *transpose*
20   ex, R in
20   prae se ferebatur, C se praeferebatur G Lb praeferebatur
21   religiosis, C G Lb R (*JB CC*) regionis Dy *omits* Db (*JB BM*) religionis
23   adoptauerat, R adoptauit

      Sanctus uero Eadwardus in regni solio sublimatus, a rege regum Domino in omni uia iustitiae et ueritatis diregebatur, cuius et auxilio fretus magno animi ingenio et sum/ma humilitate in dies crescebat. Nam in nouiter adepto honore mox pristinae probitati haec suarum incrementa uirtutum accumulauit, iuuenum uidelicet et minus sapientum consilia postponere, praedicti archipraesulis monitis mentem salubriter intendere, et secundum consilium eius et aliorum religiosorum spectabiliumque uirorum sua iudicia in omnibus exercere. Paternarum quoque traditionum aemulator fortissimus effectus, et tam in militari uirtute quam in ecclesiasticis negotiis disponendis deuote et strenue intentus, contra hostes et male agentes quadam crudelitate utebatur. Pie uiuentes uero et praecipue in sacris ordinibus constitutos sollerti cura, ueluti a patre piissimo didicerat, ab omni infestatione protegebat. Praeterea etiam quendam cotidianae consuetudinis ritum agebat, inopes alere, pauperes recreare, nudis uestimenta largiri, pro magno utique lucro ea computans, quae in tali opere consumpsisset. Tunc in Anglorum populo magna ubique extitit iocunditas, magna pacis constantia, magna rerum opulentia; quam rex eorum talibus in primo adhuc iuuentutis flore principiis deditus, cunctis erat affabilis, castitate laudabilis, facie decorus et hilaris, consilio et prudentia probatissimus.

      Sed totius bonitatis inimicus diabolus felicibus actibus inuidens, et communia regni totius gaudia disturbare cupiens, nouercam eius Ælftrid in odium ipsius concitat; cuius praesumptuosa calliditas quam sit execrabilis, ex euentu rei satis animaduerti potest, nam inuidiae zelo succensa, cogitare coepit qualiter uirum Dei a regno

1 uero, Dy *omits*
2 iustitiae, Db *omits* iu
2 ueritatis, Dy ueritate
4 in nouiter, Dy gnauiter
4 haec, Dy suae
6 sapientum, Db G R sapientium
7 mentem, C mente
9 Paternarum *to* protegebat (14) Ln *omits*
9 fortissimus, Lb (*lectionaries*) feruentissimus
11 quadam *to* et (12), C *omits*
12-13 ordinibus constitutos, C Dy G Lb R *transpose*
14 infestatione, Sj infestatitione
14 Praeterea *to* consumpsisset (17), Dy *omits*
15 agebat, Ln habebat
17 in Anglorum, Dy *omits* in
19 quam, Dy cum
19 flore, *only in* Lb *and lectionaries*
19 principiis, C principium Dy principio
22 felicibus actibus, C felicibus eius actibus Lb (*lectionaries*) felicibus actibus eius
24 cuius praesumptuosa, Lb (*lectionaries*) cuius mulieris praesumptuosa uersucia
25 satis, Lb (*lectionaries*) facile
26 succensa, Lb (*lectionaries*) *add* et diuinis humana praeponens

exstirparet, ut filius suus Æthelredus liberius in regno substitueretur.
Talia itaque ea diu in animo pertractante, / quibusdam principibus consiliariis suis secreta cordis sui aperiens, consilium super hoc cum illis habuit, orans et obtestans ut ei una assensum praeberent, et quo ordine id fieri posset excogitarent. Qui protinus in nece illius omnes consenserunt, et ut hoc quantocius perficerent fraudulenta machinatione meditabantur.

Quid multa? Confirmato ut supradiximus uenerabili uiro in regno cum iam tribus tantum annis et octo mensibus sceptro hereditario potiretur, forte die quadam cum canibus et equitibus uenandi gratia in siluam accessit, quae iuxta uillam quae dicitur Werham admodum grandis tunc habebatur, sed nunc rara tantum spineta nucumque arbores neglecto situ campis late patentibus ibi cernuntur. Ubi cum aliquamdiu incepto negotio insisteret, reminiscens fratris sui adolescentis Æthelredi, ad uisendum illum ire disposuit, quia eum puro et sincero corde diligebat.

Erat autem iuxta eandem siluam domus nouercae suae in qua praedictus puer nutriebatur, in loco qui ab incolis Corph nuncupatur, a uilla memorata tribus milibus distans, ubi nunc castrum satis celebre constructum est. Ad quam dum assumpto pauco secum comitatu proficisceretur, ecce subito in medio uiae spatio, hominibus illius ludentium more huc illucque dispersis et uagantibus, ipse absque ullo comite remansit. At ille, ut erat, solus ad domum illam, quia iam eminus eam aspiciebat, tanquam agnus mansuetissimus tendit, neminem uerens aut pertimescens, qui nec in minimis quidem aliquem se offendisse recognoscebat.

Cui dum approximaret, nuntiatum est impiissimae reginae a

2 Talia *to* multa (8), Dy *omits*
5 nece, Lb (*lectionaries*) necem
8 Quid multa, Ln *omits*
8 Confirmato, Dy *adds* itaque
9 tribus tantum, Db *transposes*
9 octo, Dy septem
11 siluam, Lb silua
11 uillam quae, Ln *omits* quae
11 dicitur, Lb uocatur (? *marginal correction to* dicitur)
12 tunc, Dy *omits*
12 nucumque, Dy ?miricumque
13 neglecto, R neglecta
15 illum, Db eum
19 celebre, Sj celeste
22 dispersis, C Sj dispersi
22 ipse absque ullo comite, Dy solus
23 ad domum *to* approximaret (27), Dy reminiscens fratris ad domum nouercae appropinquabat tanquam agnus mansuetus
24 agnus, Lb angnus
27 Cui, Lb Qui
27 nuntiatum, Dy nuntiatumque

41r mi/nistris suis illuc regem Eadwardum aduenire. Illa autem plena iniqua cogitatione et dolo, ad explenda nequitiae suae desideria adipisci se tempus idoneum gaudens, obuia mox cum satellitibus iniquitatis tanquam de aduentu eius congratulans procedit, blande eum et amicabiliter salutat, ad hospitium inuitat. Qui renuit, sed fratrem suum se uidere et alloqui uelle denuntiat: cum illa rursum ad alia se commenta transformans, iubet absque dilatione sibi potum propinari, scilicet ex occulto opperiens, ut dum ille potum incaute degustaret, opportunius quod cogitarat expleret. Interim unus etiam qui et animo audacior et scelere immanior erat, ficta dilectione Iude traditoris Domini factum imitans, pacis ei libauit osculum, ut uidelicet omnem suspicionem auferens amoremque intimum ei demonstrans, facilius suffocaret. Quod et factum est. Nam postquam poculum a pincerna suscipiens summo tenus ore attigit, is qui osculum sibi intulerat, ex aduerso insiliens, cultello mox eius uiscera transfixit. Qui graui inflictus uulnere, cum paululum inde diuertisset, de equo cui insederat subito in terram exanimis ruit. Sicque carus Dei occumbens, pro terrenis mutuauit caelestia, pro corona caduca et momentanea diadema inmarcescibile percepit aeternae felicitatis.

 Actum est autem hoc anno uerbi incarnati nongentesimo octogesimo primo, quodque dictu nefas est quadragesimali tempore, scilicet quintodecimo kalendas Aprilis. Quod, ut credimus, ad cumulanda militis sui merita diuina dispensatio sic praeordinauit: ut qui se annuo quadragesimae ieiunio carnem suam macerando
41v aliisque bonis operibus in/haerendo secundum laudabilem Christianorum ritum ad superuenturam dominicae resurrectionis diem

 1 illuc *to* aduenire, Dy illuc aduenire regem
 1 plena, Db *omits*
 3 adipisci *to* gaudens, Dy *omits*
 5 salutat, Db *adds* et
 7 absque, Dy *adds* ulla
 9 cogitarat, Dy cogitabat G cogitaret
 9 Interim. R Interea
 12 intimum ei, Db Dy Lb (*lectionaries*) *transpose*
 13 et, Dy *omits*
 14 osculum, Dy poculum
 16 graui, Lb (*lectionaries*) *omit*
 16 inflictus, Dy inflictus *corrected to* afflictus
 18 mutuauit caelestia, C mutauit R *transposes*
 20 est, Lb *adds* igitur
 20 autem, Dy *omits*
 20-21 octogesimo, Dy *omits*
 23 merita diuina, C praemia diuina (merita *added interlineally*)
 23 dispensatio sic, Ln *transposes*
 24 quadragesimae, Dy quadragesimali
 26 superuenturam, C subuenturam

praeparauerat, in bono fine consummatus, cum ipso fructu bonorum operum in caelesti curia a Christo susciperetur; quia iuxta sententiam ipsius districti iudicis in quo quisque fine deprehensus fuerit, in ipso diiudicandus erit.

Praedicta uero Ælftrid de equo illum cecidisse audiens, nequitiae suae nondum rabie exsaturata rapi corpus eius quantocius iubet et in domicilium quoddam quod iuxta erat proici, ne palam fieret quod fecerat. Cuius imperio ministri parentes nefandissimi ilico accurrunt, praedictum sacrum corpus more beluino per pedes abstrahunt, et in domicilium contemptibiliter ut iusserat proiectum uilibus stramentis cooperiunt.

Erat autem in eadem domuncula mulier quaedam a natiuitate caeca, quam memorata regina in elemosina sua pascere solebat. Quae dum sequenti nocte ibi cum sacro corpore sola pernoctasset, ecce intempesta nocte gloria Domini in eadem domo apparens, immenso eam repleuit splendore. Vnde praedicta paupercula non modico perculsa terrore, cum omnipotentis Dei misericordiam attentius deprecaretur, superna largiente gratia lumen diu desideratum meritis uiri Dei recipere meruit. Quo in loco etiam postea a fidelibus in testimonium miraculi ob eius memoriam ecclesia fabricata est, quae usque ad tempora nostra perdurauit.

Interea rumpente diluculo tenebras, dum per mulierculam illam regina quod factum fuerat comperisset, et eam quam a natiuitate

---

1-2   fructu bonorum operum, Dy bonorum operum fructu
2   a Christo susciperetur, Dy susciperetur a christo Ln *omits* a Christo
2   quia *to* erit (4), Dy *omits*
3   ipso, G christo
4   diiudicandus, Db iudicandus
5   equo, G quo
5   audiens, Dy *adds* et
7   palam fieret, G *transposes*
8   accurrunt, C accurrertur
9   more beluino, Dy *transposes*
9   abstrahunt, Db ? aitrahunt
11   cooperiunt, Dy cooperuit Ln cooperuerunt
13   sua, C *omits* R *adds interlineally*
13   solebat, C consueuerat
14   ibi, C sibi
17   modico, Lb modica
18   attentius deprecaretur, Lb *transposes*
18   gratia, G clementia
18-19   desideratum, Sj disideratum
19   Dei, C *omits*
20   testimonium, Dy Lb testimonio
21   quae *to* perdurauit, Ln *omits*
21   ad, G *omits*
21   perdurauit, R perdurat
21   Dy *adds* (N)isi granum frumenti Dy *ends here*

lumine priuatam nouerat iam illuminatam uidisset, angustiatur uultu et mente in diuersa mutatur, metuens opus suum execrabile sic posse propalari, si non attentius uiri Dei corpus tolleretur. Imperat itaque / celeriter satellitibus clanculo illud efferri, et in locis abditis et palustribus ubi minus putaretur humo tegi, ne ab aliquo amplius inueniri potuisset. Quibus iussa sine mora complentibus, edictum quo nil inclementius proposuit, ne quis de interitu eius gemeret aut omnino loqueretur, se nimirum memoriam eius de terra omnino delere existimans. His ita peractis, ad quandam sui iuris mansionem, a praedicto loco decem miliariis distantem quae Bere uocatur, continuo secessit, ut uidelicet quod fecerat sic dissimulando super hoc de ea suspicionem nemo haberet.

Interea tantus dolor filium suum Æthelredum de tam crudeli fratris sui morte inuasit, ut consolationem a nemine recipere, neque luctu neque lacrimis temperare potuisset. Vnde mater eius in furorem accensa, candelis quia aliud ad manus non habebat, atrociter eum uerberauit, ut ita ululatum eius per multa uerbera tandem compesceret. Hinc ut fertur postea toto uitae suae tempore candelas ita exosas habuit, ut uix eas aliquando coram se lucere permitteret.

Post haec igitur transacto paene anno, cum iam supernae pietati emeritum martyrem suum Eadwardum mundo innotescere, quantique meriti apud se fuerit declarare complacuisset, corpus eius uenerabile quibusdam fidelibus deuote quaerentibus reuelare dignatus est, atque caelesti indicio demonstrare. Nam circa locum ipsum ubi occultatum fuerat, columna instar ignis desuper emissa apparuit, quae lucis suae radiis locum undique frequenter irradiare uisa est. Quod quidam uiri deuoti de uilla uicina Werham uidentes, congregati in unum de memorato loco illud sustulerunt, et in uillam suam deportauerunt. Fit interim concursus ingens et planctus omnium regias / exequias prosequentium, uox una ululantium. "Heu" inquiunt "quid iam post haec solacii sperare poterimus? Quis nos ab hostium

2 posse, Lb *omits*
3 propalari, A *begins again here*
8 se, C G Lb R sic
9 His *to* permitteret (19), Ln *omits*
9 ita, C itaque
11 fecerat, G *adds* ut uidelicet
13 tam, G tanti
14 fratris sui morte, R morte fratris sui
17 ita, C sic
18 Hinc, Db Hic
18 fertur, C G R (?Lb) ferunt
18 ita, Db *omits*
20 transacto paene, Ln *transposes*
21 suum, G filium
22 meriti apud se, C apud se meriti
25 occultatum, R occultum

incursionibus percusso tam dulcissimo pastore liberabit? Periere gaudia nostra, immo et patriae nostrae pacis et concordiae foedera confusa sunt." Tunc cum his gementium uocibus ad ecclesiam sanctae Dei genitricis Mariae corpus uenerabile perductum, ad orientalem eius plagam officiosissime die iduum mensis Februarii sepelierunt, ubi lignea ecclesiola, quae postea a uiris religiosis fabricata est, usque hodie demonstratur. Fons etiam in loco in quo prius iacuerat, dulces et perspicuas aquas ex eo tempore usque hodie emanare cernitur, nomenque eius a sancti uiri nomine adaptatum fons sancti Eadwardi dicitur, ubi infirmis multa cotidie ad laudem Domini nostri Iesu Christi praestantur beneficia.

Interea fama uulgante per uniuersam Anglorum patriam fraus et impietas reginae manifestatur, regis innocentis praeconium extollitur, uirtutum et meritorum eius insignia ubique praedicantur. Audiens itaque quidam comes magnificus, Ælfere nomine, sanctum corpus tam praeclaro indicio inuentum, immenso perfusus gaudio, dominoque suo tanquam adhuc uiuo fidele obsequium praebere desiderans, in digniorem locum illud transferre decreuit. Erat enim idem uir illustris magnam de crudeli eius interitu compassionem habens, et nimis indigne ferens tam pretiosam margaritam in tam uili loco obfuscari. Ad quod opus digne peragendum, episcopos et abbates cum optimatibus regni quos habere potuit inuitat, et ut in hoc sibi negotio consentiant et subueniant monet, precatur. Nuntium quoque ad abbatissam Wilfridam in monasterio quod Wiltonia uocatur dirigit, et ut ad peragendas tanti uiri exe/quias cum sibi commissis uirginibus conueniat denuntiat.

Erat autem in eodem monasterio quaedam uenerabilis uirgo, soror ipsius sancti, magna uitae et morum honestate pollens, Edgit nunc-

---

² nostrae, Lb totius
5-6 ubi lignea *to* demonstratur (7), Ln *omits*
⁶ ecclesiola, R ecclesia
⁶ quae, Lb *omits here, inserts after* est
⁹ Eadwardi, R *omits*
¹⁰ multa, Lb *omits*
10-11 Iesu Christi, R *omits*
¹³ impietas, G impietatis
¹⁴ praedicantur, C prae praedicatur
¹⁵ quidam, Lb *omits*
¹⁵ corpus, Lb *adds* eius
¹⁷ in, R ad
¹⁸ illud transferre *to* sexus (9,30), Ln *compresses*
¹⁹ compassionem, A copassionem
²¹ obfuscari, G effuscari
²² potuit, R poterat
²⁴ Wiltonia, Lb Wiltun
²⁵ ad, A G *omit*

upata, quae supradicti regis gloriosissimi Edgari et eiusdem Wilfridae, nondum Deo consecratae, filia fuerat. Quibus mox cum summa diligentia et ueneratione conuenientibus episcopis quoque cum abbatibus, ut diximus, congregatis, praedictus Ælfere ex Dorsata non modicam uirorum ac mulierum multitudinem coadunauit, et ad Werham ubi corpus uiri Dei sepulturae traditum fuerat, cum magna deuotione peruenit. Quod protinus in conspectu totius populi detectum et a terra extractum, ita ab omni corruptione illaesum inuentum est ac si eodem die tumulatum fuisset. Videntes autem hoc episcopi ceterique ordinis uiri, in hymnis et laudibus omnipotentis Dei misericordiam glorificauerunt, qui emeriti martyris sui innocentiam tali indicio dignatus est demonstrare. Praedicta uero uirgo soror ipsius accurrens, corpus desideratissimum amplectitur, sanctis fouet manibus, oscula ingerit. Lacrimarum largis humectationibus faciem rigat, tum gemitibus, tum spirituali gaudio de tanta fratris gloria mentem nequit explere. Tunc a uenerabilium uirorum manibus susceptum et feretro impositum, cum magno cleri et plebis tripudio ad Scephtoniam deducitur, quia idem coenobium in honore sanctae Dei genitricis Mariae dedicatum admodum celebre habebatur.

Fuerat enim a diuae memoriae Ælfredo rege magnifico, qui erat atauus ipsius sancti uiri, decentissime ex ea occasione constructum, quia idem rex filiam quandam habens, Aileuam nomine, eamque

43v sponso caelesti desponsare cupiens, monasticis disci/plinis mancipatam in eadem ecclesia tradiderat, pro cuius amore plurimis frequenter et largis muneribus illam nobilitauit. Nam inter reliqua donorum suorum insignia, centum hidas terrae ita quietas et liberas sicut ipse eas melius tenuerat in perpetuum possidendas ei condonauit, quarum usque hodie uirgines inibi Christo famulantes experiuntur beneficia.

Interea cum undique uulgus utriusque sexus ad tam insolitam rem ex diuersis locis confluxisset, duo etiam pauperes, tanta acerbitate

2   Deo, R *omits*
5   et, Db ut
7   in, Db *omits*
7-8 a terra extractum, Lb extractum a terra
9   autem hoc, Lb *omits*
9   ceterique, Lb *adds* sacri
12   uero, Lb quoque
12   uirgo, Lb *adds* uenerabilis
13   desideratissimum, C Db Lb desiderantissimum (n *added in* C *interlineally*)
15   mentem, C mente G mortem
17   feretro, Lb *adds* deuote
17   plebis tripudio, G *transposes*
18   sanctae, G beate
18   Dei genitricis, G *omits*
27   in perpetuum, C imperpetuum
31   ex diuersis locis, Ln *omits*

morbi contracti ita ut uix per terram manibus cruribusque repere possent, inter ceteros aduenere, Dominum sanctumque Eadwardum pro sua incommoditate rogaturi. Qui feretro approximantes, cum ii qui sacrum corpus ferebant super eos pro recuperanda sospitate illud deportassent, statim in conspectu populi sanitati restituti sunt. Quo uiso, clamor populi in altum extollitur, merita sancti Eadwardi omnes in commune uenerantur.

Regina quoque memorata interim audiens quae per uirum sanctum fiebant magnalia, compuncta super iis quae fecerat, equo mox ascenso post eum pro commisso suo ueniam rogatura disposuit ire. Minime sibi diuina ui resistente concessum est; nam dum in itinere cum suis equitaret satellitibus, ecce miro quodam et inestimabili impedimento ita detinebatur, ut equus super quem sedebat retrorsum potius quam in ante uersa uice intenderet. Quem freno constringere uolens cum interdum hac interdum uero illac diuertendo neque minis neque uerberibus proficere potuisset, animaduertit peccatis suis exigentibus sic se detineri. Vnde ilico de equo in terra prosiliens, tamquam ob maiorem reuerentiam pedes ire parat, / sed iterum, quod dictu mirabile est, retorta nihilominus quod concupierat consequi ualuit, ut uidelicet aperte clareret, pro scelere quod in uirum Dei operata est haec sibi euenire.

Interea perductum uenerabile corpus ad memoratum coenobium, et a uirginibus inibi Deo seruientibus digne et laudabiliter receptum, in septentrionali parte arae principalis cum magno honore duodecimo kalendas Martii tumulatur, ubi multa beneficia per eum infirmis post haec diuina largita est clementia.

1   ita, Lb Ln *omit*
1   repere, G reperere
3   incommoditate, R incolumitate
3   ii, C iis
8   sanctum, Lb dei
9   magnalia, G miracula
10 disposuit ire, Lb *transposes* C G Lb Ln R *add* sed
12 et, Ln *omits*
12 inestimabili, Lb ineffabili
14 ante, Lb antea
14 intenderet, Lb incederet
17 in terra, C G Lb R (*JB*) in terram Ln *omits*
18 pedes, Ln pede
18 dictu, C dictum
19 consequi, G Lb R *add* non
20 haec sibi, Ln *transposes*
22 perductum, Sj productum
23 a, C *omits*
24 parte, C *omits*
24 principalis, Ln principali
24 duodecimo, C duodecim

Quaedam namque matrona in remotis Angliae partibus degens, cum nimia debilitate grauaretur, et cotidie pro sua incolumitate preces in conspectu piissimi opificis Dei funderet, nocte quadam ei sanctus Eadwardus in uisu astitit, cui et talia dixisse fertur. "Cum diliculo surrexeris, ad locum ubi sepulturae traditus sum ire ne differas, quia illic noua calciamenta infirmitati tuae necessaria recipies." Erat enim ut ex coniectura colligere possumus in pedibus grauius collisa, ideoque per calciamenta noua sanitas pedum designabatur. Euigilans autem mane, cum somnium quod uiderat cuidam uicinae suae retulisset, illa uisionis incredula, phantasma esse asserebat. Interea uero cum monitis sancti praedicta matrona parere dissimularet, adest rursus ei uir sanctus in uisione dicens, "Quare, praecepta mea respuens, tantopere salutem tuam negligis? Vade ergo ad sepulchrum meum et ibi liberaberis." Illa autem resumptis uiribus dixit ad eum, "Et quis es tu. domine? Aut ubi sepulchrum tuum inueniam?" Cui ille, "Ego", inquit, "sum rex Eadwardus iniusta nuper nece peremptus, 44v et Scephtoniae in ecclesia / beatae Dei genitricis Mariae sepultus." Mulier autem mane euigilans, et quod uiderat secum reputans, assumptis mox quae in itinere necessaria fuerant, ad monasterium praedictum tendit; ibique tandem perueniens, cum aliquamdiu Deum sanctumque Eadwardum humili corde exoraret, sanitati restituta est.

Praeterea quoque ad tumbam uiri Dei plurima frequenter patrata sunt miracula, quae negligentia scriptorum memoriae litterarum minime tradita sunt. Verum nos reticere maluimus, quam de sancto uiro alia quam quae fideliter scripta repperimus, aut quae fidelium relatione didicimus, inconsiderate diceremus. Vnde his omissis, qualiter eius sacratissimae reliquiae de terra leuatae sint paucis aperiemus. Igitur cum iam merita gloriosi martyris Eadwardi, miraculorum magnalibus quae cotidie ad tumbam eius fiebant, longe

1 Quaedam *to* aperiemus (28), Ln *omits*
3 piissimi, R pii
10 Interea, Lb Interim
11 adest, Lb *omits*
12 uisione, Lb *adds* apparuit
17 Dei genitricis Mariae, G marie dei genitricis
19 assumptis, G assumptus
20 praedictum, Sj *omits*
20 ibique *to* dispensationi (12,1), A *mutilated*
21 sanctumque, A *omits* que Db et sanctum Sj *adds* que *interlineally*
22 patrata sunt miracula, Lb miracula patrata sunt
23 memoriae litterarum minime, Lb minime memorie
24 maluimus, quam, C maluimus, quod
25 fideliter, G fidelitas
26 relatione, Lb rescripta
26 Vnde *to* aperiemus (28), Lb *omits*
26 omissis, G comissis

lateque declararentur, et supernae iam dispensationi ut eius sacrae reliquiae a terra leuarentur complacuisset, coepit hoc quibusdam indiciis ipse sanctus manifestare, et quo ordine id fieri debuisset uisionibus quibusdam demonstrare. Nam tumulus in quo requiescebat tanta in dies facilitate a terra eleuabatur, ut liquido cunctis appareret, eum a loco illo uelle transferri.

Praeterea quoque cuidam uiro religioso in uisione apparuit, cui et dixit, "Vade ad coenobium quod famoso nomine Scephtonia uocatur, et ad uirginem Æthelfredam quae ceteris inibi Deo famulantibus praeest perfer mandata. Dices ergo ei quia in loco in quo nunc iaceo diutius esse nolo, et ut hoc fratri meo absque aliqua dilatione denuntiet ex mea parte impera." Qui mane consurgens, et diuinam quam uiderat uisionem intelligens, ad abbatissam ut iussus fuerat concite tendit, cuncta quae ostensa sibi fuerant / per ordinem ei retulit. At illa, super hoc omnipotenti Deo gratias agens, uniuersa protinus auribus regis Æthelredi exposuit, sed et sepulchri eius eleuationem cum summa deuotione innotuit. Audiens autem rex tantam fratris sui gloriam, immenso perfunditur gaudio, et libenter quidem, si opportunitas daretur, ad tale eius praeconium conueniret, libenter eleuationi eius interesse desideraret. Sed quam uariis et grauibus hostium incursionibus circumquaque uallatus, praesentiam suam ad id peragendum minime exhibere potuit. Nuntios ad reuerentissimum Wilsinum, Sireburnensem episcopum, et ad quendam magnae sanctitatis praesulem, Elfsinum nomine, ceterosque uenerabilis uitae uiros dirigit, monens et imperans ut fratris sui corpus de terra eleuatum condigno loco reponerent. Qui secundum regium mandatum ad supradictum monasterium cum innumerabili uirorum ac mulierum

1   declararentur, G declararantur   1-2   sacrae reliquiae, Lb *transposes*
3   debuisset, Sj debuissent
4   requiescebat, C et quiescebat
5   facilitate, C felicitate
7   uiro religioso, Lb *transposes*
7   uisione, R (*NLA*) sompnis
8   Vade *to* Deo (15) A *mutilated*
8   famoso, G famosa
9   Deo, Ln *omits*
10 praeest, Lb *adds* mea
10 perfer, Ln *adds* mea
11 aliqua, Lb *omits*
14 tendit, Lb *adds* et
14 ostensa sibi, Lb *transposes*
15 omnipotenti, Ln *omits*
16 Æthelredi, G *adds* fratris eius
17 tantam, G tanto
18 et, Lb *omits*
24 Elfsinum *to* nebulae (13,4), A *mutilated*
25 de terra eleuatum, G eleuatum de terra
26 loco, Db loculo
27 monasterium, R locum

turba libenti animo conuenientes, aperto cum summa ueneratione monumento, tanta ex eo odoris fragrantia emanauit, ut omnes qui aderant in Paradisi deliciis se constitutos aestimarent; unde etiam in tantum tota ecclesia repleta est, ut in modum nebulae candentis appareret. Tunc pontifices gloriosissimi deuote accedentes, de tumulo sacras reliquias sustulerunt, et in locello ad hoc diligenter preparato eas componentes, in sancta sanctorum cum aliis sanctorum reliquiis in spirituali diuinae exultationis tripudio intulerunt. Eleuatum est itaque sacratissimum corpus eius anno uicesimo primo ex quo illic tumulatum fuerat, qui erat annus ab incarnatione Domini millesimus primus, regnante eodem Domino nostro Iesu Christo, qui cum Patre et Spiritu Sancto uiuit et gloriatur Deus per omnia saecula saeculorum, Amen. /

45v EXPLICIT PASSIO. INCIPIUNT MIRACULA INTERUENTU EUISDEM PATRATA.

Plurima miracula per sanctum Eadwardum patrata sunt, de quibus pauca huic nostro opusculo inserere curauimus. Temporibus igitur regis gloriosissimi Eadwardi, qui fuerat supra memorati regis Æthelredi filius, nepos uidelicet sancti Eadwardi, erat in trans-

---

2 odoris, Lb *adds* suauissimi
3 aderant, R affuerant
3 unde, Lb inde
6 sacras, Lb *omits*
6 reliquias, A C G Ln R Sj delicias
6 sustulerunt, G distulerunt
6 diligenter, Ln decenter (*NLA* ad locum decentiorem)
6-7 diligenter preparato eas, C *omits* eas R preparato eas diligenter
8 reliquiis, C G Lb R *add* uenerandis
8 in, Ln R cum
8 Eleuatum, Ln Eleuatumque
9 eius, R *omits*
9 primo, Ln *omits*
9 quo, G *omits*
11 nostro, G *omits*
12 Patre *to* talis (14,3), A *mutilated*
12 uiuit *to* patrata (14), C *omits*
12 gloriatur, Db Ln regnat
13 Amen, G *ends here*
14 Explicit *to* patrata, A (Ex)plicit passio sancti ead(uua)rdi regis et martyris. (Inci)piunt miracula (e)iusdem Db Explicit passio sancti eadwardi regis. Incipiunt miracula eiusdem Ln Explicit de sancto edwardo rege Anglorum et martire Ln *ends here* R *omits*
14-15 Explicit *to* patrata sunt, Lb Post hec quoque plurima per eundem uirum dei miracula in eadem ecclesia patrata sunt
16 nostro opusculo, Lb *transposes*
16 Temporibus, Lb Tempore
17 regis gloriosissimi, Db Lb *transpose*
18 in, Lb *omits*

marinis partibus in pago Viromandensi uir quidam, Iohannes nomine, degens, qui cruciatu graui ita toto corpore contractus fuerat, ut talis eius renibus coniunctis, ad nulla penitus membrorum officia se erigere posset. Hic itaque in uisione nocturna admonitus est, ut in Angliam pergens ad monasterium Scephtoniam, in quo sanctus Eadwardus requiescebat, tenderet, quia illic sanitatem recepturus esset. Quod dum uicinis et cognatis suis retulisset, consilio et auxilio eorum fretus mare transiens, ad coenobium memoratum post diuersa locorum diuerticula tandem peruenit; ubi dum aliquanto tempore pro reddenda sibi sospitate Deum sanctumque Eadwardum deprecaretur, sanitati restitutus est. Qui etiam in eodem monasterio postea seruiens usque ad extremum uitae suae tempus permansit, de quo omnes paene ibi manentes qui eum uiderunt usque hodie testimonium perhibent.

Nec multo post, quidam leprosus ad memoriam eiusdem sancti ueniens, cum in orationibus et uigiliis pro sua infirmitate diuinum inuocaret auxilium, ab omni leprae spurcitia mundatus est.

46r Aliud etiam miraculum post haec interiecto aliquanti temporis spatio per eundem uirum uenerabilem contigit, quod relatione spectabilium personarum quae hoc uiderunt didicimus. Cum enim uir uenerabilis Heremannus, Salesberiensis episcopus ecclesiae, quodam tempore episcopii sui parochias pia curiositate circumiret, et ad memoratum coenobium Scephtoniam uisitandi gratia diuertisset, pauper quidam quem in elemosina sua pascere solitus erat in comitatu suo aduenit. Fuerat enim haec eiusdem gloriosi pontificis pia consuetudo, ut ubicumque more cotidiano iter arriperet, cum eo semper nonnulli debiles et infirmi eius alimonia reficiendi ducerentur. Qui dum apud praefatum monasterium aliquamdiu moram fecisset, memoratus caecus, ductu pueri a quo gressus eius dirigebatur, ecclesiam oraturus intrauit. Vbi dum pro sua incommoditate omnipotentis Dei pietatem deuote implorando, orationis cursum usque in uesperum protraheret, custodes in ecclesia diligentiam facientes,

1 Viromandensi, A, Lb uiromadensi
1-2 Iohannes nomine, Lb *transposes*
2 graui, Lb grauissimo
11 deprecaretur, Db precaretur
18 Aliud *to* Salesberiensis (21), A *mutilated*
19 uirum uenerabilem, Lb *transposes*
21 episcopus ecclesiae, Db *omits* ecclesiae Lb *transposes*
22 sui, R *omits*
22 circumiret, Db Sj circuiret
24 pauper quidam, A *transposes*
24 solitus erat, A *omits* erat Lb *solebat*
29 dirigebatur, C dirigebantur
31 pietatem deuote, Lb *transposes*
31 cursum, Lb cursus

14

eumque orationi deditum reperientes, egredi illum hortantur, sed ille nequaquam se egressurum, immo misericordiam Dei sanctique Eadwardi illic sese expectaturum constanter profitetur. Quod illi audientes et fidem hominis admirantes, eum in oratione iacere permittunt, puerum uero eius ad hospitium suum redire compellunt. Interea dum in loco illo aliquamdiu requiesceret, primo ingenti perfusus frigore, dein calore immenso corpore toto correptus lumen recepit. Quod dum mane diuulgatum fuisset, ii quibus sanior mens inerat, nequaquam facile ad credendum persuaderi poterant, donec illi qui eum prius nouerant interrogati sub testimonio ueritatis illum ex multo tempore caecum fuisse affirmarent. Tunc praecepto episcopi 46v in ecclesia uirgines inibi Deo / famulantes cum populorum concursionibus congregatae, in hymnis et laudibus signis interim pulsantibus Christo laudum praeconia exsoluerunt, qui haec meritis sancti Eadwardi operari dignatus est.

Quidam itidem homo grauibus ob peccatorum suorum commissa ferri ligaminibus uinculatus, dum post haec in eadem ecclesia tanto deuotius, quanto acriori constringebatur dolore, in conspectu maiestatis Dei preces funderet, meritis uiri Dei liberari meruit.

Praeterea quoque plurima per merita ipsius frequenter patrata sunt magnalia, quae litterarum apicibus minime tradita sunt. Verum omnipotenti Domino, qui solus facit mirabilia, melius ea commendantes, ad eum finem orationis conuertamus.

Subueniant itaque nobis, piissime aeterni regis miles Eadwarde, tua sancta patrocinia, nostraeque imperfectioni condescendens, tuis piis deprecationibus obtine apud misericordissimum iudicem ut nulla nos humanae iactantiae inflatio deiciat, nulla nos libidinum inquinamenta a castissimis caelestis sponsi amplexibus separent, nullae

1 egredi *to* iacere (4), A *mutilated*
2 immo, Lb *adds* in
2 sanctique, Db et sancti
4 eum in oratione, Db in oratione eum
7 corpore toto, Db *transposes*
8 fuisset, Lb esset
9 persuaderi, C prosuaderi
11 praecepto, C Lb R ex praecepto
13 interim, C iterum, Lb *adds* insimul
14 haec, A hoc
18 constringebatur dolore, Lb *transposes*
19 liberari, Lb *adds* pro
20 Praeterea, R Propterea
20 frequenter patrata, Db *transposes*
25 nostraeque, Db *omits* que
26-27 nulla nos, Lb *transposes*
27 libidinum, R libidinis
28 separent, Sj separant

uitiorum sordes actus nostros occupent; sed te opitulante semper ad caelestia desideria subleuemur, ut quandoque tecum et cum omnibus sanctis perpetuis deliciis in caelesti Ierusalem perfrui mereamur; praestante Domino nostro Iesu Christo, qui cum aeterno Patre et amborum Spiritu Sancto uiuit et regnat Deus, per immortalia saecula saeculorum, Amen.

4 aeterno, C R co-aeterno
5 immortalia *to* Amen, A *mutilated*. A *adds* Expliciunt (mi)racula sancti eaduuar(di re)gis et martyris Db *adds* Expliciunt miracula sancti Eadwardi martiris R *adds* Explicit uita sancti edwardi regis et martiris

APPENDIX A

    MS BM Harley 1117
1r Omnibus est recolenda dies qua maximus anglum
    Sternitur eadweardus dira rex morte peremptus.
    Inuidia certum est propria quem gente necatum.   3
    Tres annos et dimidium qui rexerat anglos.
    Heu ueriti nec sunt domini sic fallere dextram.
    Nam iunctus superis Christum quaesiuit in astris.   6
    Tempore post paruo fruitur fulcimine honesto.
    Auxilio Christi nullo dubitamine fungens:
    Tollitur e tumulo iacuit quo conditus ante   9
    Subuehitur feretro digne comitante popello.
    At iuxta primi procerum multique ierarchi.
    Aelfere quos interfuerat dignissimus archos.   12
    Tunc urbem capiunt sceftei quae burg uocitatur.
    Fit gemitus. longosque cient precordia fletus.
    Iura sepulturae statuunt. laudesque frequentant.   15
    Redditur atque solo corpus. et flamen olimpho.
    Angelicoque choro transuectus calle secundo
    Nunc penetrat caelos sparsit quia sanguine terras.   18
    Per carnis iugulum meruit conscendere caelum.
    O felix nimium carnis ergastola linquens
    Nam satis aegregiam sumpsit pro funere palmam: 21
    Carmine composito factum quod poscerat ordo
    Nunc finem facimus scribendi pollice uersus.
    Te frater rogito quamuis non grammate compto   24
    Sint cunctis secreta modis sintagmatis acta
    Funde preces pro quo sedes rogitamine summo:

9   ante, *followed by* n. *perhaps having been read as* amen
22   Carmine, *preceded by marginal red initial* K

APPENDIX B

     MS Cambridge, Corpus Christi 371
3r Aue dies pręfulgida. in qua superna curia. Congaudet & dignissimam. Regi deo dat gloriam. / Mira dei bonitas. mira potentia. Quę bona cuncta creans ordinat omnia. aequo moderamine. / Regni dei clarissime Conciuis & rex anglię. Pręstans tuorum gloria. Laus & corona splendida. YMNVS DE SANCTO EADVVARDO REGE & MARTIR   3
Aue dies pręfulgida. in qua superna curia Congaudet & dignissimam. Regi deo dat gloriam. Uir nanque sęclo prępotens. & sceptra regni possidens. Iam nunc polorum gaudiis Admixtus. hęret angelis.   6
Edwardus hic uocamine. clara satus propagine. cuius manus. os. pectora. Sibi pararunt sidera. Hinc inuidorum pessima Fraus. & nouerca subdola. neci beatum subdidit. Viuumque cęlis intulit.   9
Edwarde rex suauissime. Decus tuorum nobile. coniunctus en archangelis. tuis adesto seruulis. Summo patri cum filio. Et spiritu paraclito. Sit laus. potestas. gloria. per cuncta semper secula. AMEN.   12
ITEM. Mira dei bonitas. mira potentia. Quę bona cuncta creans ordinat omnia. ęquo moderamine. Ætheris hic solium contulit inclitum Edwardo. quoniam rex fuit anglię. Iustus. pius. optimus.   15
Dunstani patris hunc os docuit sacrum. Inque dei stabilem exhibuit uia(m). Quę duxit eum deo. Quod probat esse ratum cęlitus emicans eius in exanimes corporis artus lumen uenerabile. Hinc honor atque   18
decus ingenito patri Sit genitoque patris pneumate cum sacro. per sęcla perennia. AMEN
ITEM. Regni dei clarissime conciuis & rex anglię. pręstans tuorum   21
3v gloria. laus & corona splendida. Edwar/de quem perlucidum Sidus diei perpetis lustrauit. ac sacrissima Sua beauit gratia. Tu iam nouercę fraudibus Non subiacebis amplius Sed te tenente cęlica.   24
illam premit sors ultima. Manens tibi nunc gaudium Stat. & perenne premium. Quo nos beari perpetim. Tuo precatu poscimus. Nobis pater cum filio Et spiritu paraclito. Det consequi feliciter Quod poscimus fideliter. AMEN   27

     15 secula, *expanded thus for the rhythm though not in accordance with scribal practice at 8 and 23.*
     21 in, *a dot under the* n *may indicate expunctuation.*

The music to these three hymns by Eadmer is written in Norman notation, although the neume shapes have a number of Roman characteristics. The *virga* and *punctum* are used in the normal way to indicate respectively higher and lower pitch; but this happens also in the distrophae at the word *congaudet*, which is unusual. A distropha would normally be two *virgae* in Norman notation or two *puncta* in Roman. (See Carl Parrish, *The Notation of Medieval Music* (London 1958), pp. 5 and 6.)

The second of the hymns appears to be prose, but the first and third are stanzaic. The first verse of the first hymn normalized would be:

Aue dies praefulgida
In qua superna curia
Congaudet et dignissimam
Regi Deo dat gloriam.

The third hymn follows the same pattern but the rhyme is twice broken. At 18, 25-6 *perlucidum* and *perpetis*, at 18, 29 *perpetim* and *poscimus* fail to rhyme. That a form of the same word is involved in both, suggests the way in which scribal error could have arisen.

Aue dies presulgida. in qua supna curia. congaudet & dignissimam.

Regi deo dat gloriam. Mira dei bonitas. mira potentia.

Que bona cuncta creans ordinat omnia equo moderamine.

Regni dei clarissime conciuis & rex anglie. prestans tuoy gloria

laus & corona splendida. SONUS DE SCO EDWARDO REGE 7 MARTIR

Aue dies presulgida. in qua supna curia congaudet & dignissima
Regi dō dat glam. Vir nanq; seclo prepotens. & sceptra regni
possidens. iam nc polox gaudiis admixtus. heret angelis. Edwar
dus hic uocamine. clara satus pagine. cui manus. os. pectora. sibi
pararunt sidera. Hinc inuidox pessima fraus. & nouerca subdo
la neci beatu subdidit. viuuq; celis intulit. Edwarde rex suauis
sime. decus tuox nobile. coniunct en archangelis. tuis adesto seruu
lis. Summo patri cu filio. Et spu paraclito. Sit laus. potestas. gla. p cun
cta semp scla. Aōn. Item. Mira di bonitas. mira potentia. que
bona cuncta creans ordinat omnia equo moderamine. & cleri
hic solm contulit inclitum Edwardo. qm rex fuit anglie. iustus. pius.
optimus. Dunstani patris hunc os docuit sacrū. inq; dei stabile ex
hibuit uiā. a ue dixere eū dō. Qd pbat esse ratu celitus emicans eius
in exanimes corporis artus lumen uenerabile. Hinc honor atq;
decus ingenito patri. & genito q; patris pneumate cū sacro. p
scla pennia. Aōn. Item. Regni di clarissime conciuis &
rex anglie. prestans tuox gla. laus & corona splendida. Edwar